AMERICAN JUDAISM
Adventure in Modernity

PRENTICE-HALL INTERNATIONAL, INC., *London*
PRENTICE-HALL OF AUSTRALIA, PTY. LTD., *Sydney*
PRENTICE-HALL OF CANADA, LTD., *Toronto*
PRENTICE-HALL OF INDIA PRIVATE LIMITED, *New Delhi*
PRENTICE-HALL OF JAPAN, INC., *Tokyo*

AMERICAN JUDAISM
Adventure in Modernity

JACOB NEUSNER

Brown University
Providence, Rhode Island

PRENTICE-HALL, INC., Englewood Cliffs, New Jersey

ISBN: C 0-13-027870-X
ISBN: P 0-13-027862-9

Library of Congress Catalog Card Number: 70–161677

Printed in the United States of America

10   9   8   7   6   5   4   3   2   1

PREFACE

AMERICA IS THE MODEL OF MODERNITY, and the American Jewish experience of modernity is in some ways paradigmatic of that of modern man. One dilemma of modernity is: What of tradition? Of the experience of the past? For the Jew it is this: How to mediate between the claims of classical Judaism, the work of ages of faith, archaic, supernatural, and sacred, and the ineluctable demands of contemporaneity, secularity, unbelief, and worldliness? What happens to religion beyond the age in which men take ritual for reality and myth for granted, thus tell *us fact* the stories meant to convey the essential structure of being in highly symbolic form and to reveal the truth of life? What happens to their imaginative life? How do they mediate between the claim of contemporaneity and the demands of their vast inheritance of institutions, rituals, myths and theologies, social and cultural patterns, derived from the archaic age? Clearly, that inheritance remains very present in the modern world. But what of that presence? Is it a wraith or an augury?

American Judaism supplies evocative materials for a case-study of the religious experience of modernity. When we ask, "What does it mean to be a Jew in contemporary America?" we seek a particular sort of religious and cultural datum, because we suppose that datum to be revealing, suggestive beyond itself. American Jews stand at the margins of society, and are therefore conscious of traits others take for granted. At the frontiers of culture, they moreover are clearly visible to others. So American Judaism may serve as a mirror of American religious life, and American Jews as a model of modernity.

Since our question is, "What happens to archaic religions in modern American civilization?" we adopt categories of inquiry into the traits of archaic religions developed by historians of religions—the modes of the sacred. American Judaism supplies important data for five of these categories: holy way—the pattern of everyday actions imposed by a religious tradition; holy man—the person set apart as a bearer of religious truth, grace, and supernatural power; holy people—the religious community as the locus at which the supernatural enters history; holy land—the place set apart for meaningful history; and holy faith—the doctrines and beliefs that explain and verify experienced reality. Other important questions raised by historians of religions elicit more interesting answers from data supplied by other religious groups in American society.

At the end we shall not evade the question of meaning: What is *religious* about contemporary religious life? Do we witness the last stages of the tradition's lingering demise, or the beginnings of a fundamentally new human creation?

The answers are given in anthologizing essays, which are neither anthologies nor sustained essays.

My thanks go to my students, Gary Porton, David Goodblatt, William Scott Green, David Altshuler, and Eli Hirschfeld, who read the manuscript and helped with the proofs. Brown University granted me a sabbatical leave in 1970–71, and the American Council of Learned Societies provided a research fellowship for the same period. Brown University furthermore pays the considerable costs of typing manuscripts, preparing indexes, and numerous other research expenses. I am grateful to my University for its continuing support of my work. My colleagues at Brown University are a source of intellectual challenge and support. To them, in particular, Professors Wendell S. Dietrich, Ernest Frerichs, and Horst R. Moehring, I am especially grateful. My interest in American Jewish affairs is not impersonal or objective, but occupies the very center of my life. My wife, Suzanne, shares this engagement, participates in the experience this book attempts to convey and evaluate, and, above all, is the director of our joint enterprise in American Jewish life: the nurture of our sons, Samuel Aaron, Eli Ephraim, and Noam Mordecai Menahem. If she and I, with others of our inchoate fellowship of perplexed parents, choose to affirm what might easily be deplored, the reason is the necessity imposed by our sons, the hope demanded for their future. Finally and most important, my editor at Prentice-Hall, George Coy, provoked me to return to the study of American Judaism after fifteen years of study of another place and another age, and encouraged me to address the questions before us. He has been a good counsellor and a good editor. The obvious limitations of perception and prejudice are mine alone; mine too are the errors.

The work is completed on the fifteenth wedding anniversary of my beloved friends, Avraham and Yonina Udovitch, to whom, and to whose children, the book is dedicated.

Jacob Neusner
Providence, Rhode Island

ACKNOWLEDGMENTS

THE AUTHOR IS INDEBTED to the following for permission to reprint excerpts from copyrighted material:

Yivo Institute for Jewish Research for "The Shtetl Way of Life," by Elias Tcherikower, in *The Early Jewish Labor Movement in the United States*, translated and revised by Aaron Antonovsky, © 1961 by Yivo Institute for Jewish Research; University of Chicago Press for *American Judaism* by Nathan Glazer, © 1957 by University of Chicago Press; Jewish Publication Society for "Ideologies of American Jews," by Harold Weisberg; and Arthur Hertzberg, "The American Jew and His Religion," in Oscar I. Janowsky, ed., *The American Jew: A Reappraisal,* © 1964 by Jewish Publication Society of America; Howard Singer for *Bring Forth the Mighty Men* by Howard Singer (N. Y., 1969: Funk and Wagnalls, Inc.), © 1969 by Howard Singer; American Jewish Archives for "Power in a Midwestern Jewish Community" by Kenneth D. Roseman, in *American Jewish Archives,* Vol. 21, No. 1, April, 1969, © 1969 by American Jewish Archives; Stuart E. Rosenberg for *The Search for Jewish Identity in America* by Stuart E. Rosenberg (N. Y., 1965: Doubleday Anchor), © 1965 by Stuart E. Rosenberg; Theodore Herzl Foundation and Arthur Hertzberg for "The Changing American Rabbinate," by Arthur Hertzberg, in *Midstream,* Vol. 12, No. 1, January, 1966, © 1966 by Theodore Herzl Foundation; Richard L. Rubenstein for "A Rabbi Dies," by

Richard L. Rubenstein, © 1971 by Richard L. Rubenstein; American Jewish Committee for "Reflections on Jewish Identity," by Daniel Bell, in Peter I. Rose, ed., *The Ghetto and Beyond. Essays on Jewish Life in America* (N. Y., 1969: Random House), © 1961 by American Jewish Committee; *European Journal of Sociology* for "The Rise and Decline of Anti-Semitism in America," by Dennis H. Wrong, in Peter I. Rose, ed., *The Ghetto and Beyond,* © 1965 by *European Journal of Sociology;* Will Herberg for *Protestant Catholic Jew,* by Will Herberg (N. Y., 1960: Doubleday Anchor), © 1960 by Will Herberg; American Jewish Committee for *Jewish Identity on the Suburban Frontier. A Study of Group Survival in the Open Society,* by Marshall Sklare and Joseph Greenblum (N. Y., 1967: Basic Books, Inc.), © 1967 by American Jewish Committee; Bobbs-Merrill Co. Inc. for *A Partisan Guide to the Jewish Problem* by Milton Steinberg, © 1963 by Bobbs-Merrill Co. Inc.; Jewish Publication Society and American Jewish Committee for "A Century of Jewish Immigration to the United States," by Oscar and Mary F. Handlin, in *The American Jewish Yearbook,* Vol. 50, 1948–9, © 1949 by Jewish Publication Society and American Jewish Committee; Theodore Herzl Foundation for "Zionism and 'The Jewish Problem'," by Jacob Neusner, in *Midstream,* Vol. 15, No. 9, November, 1969, © 1969 by Theodore Herzl Foundation; American Jewish Congress for "Judaism and the Zionist Problem," by Jacob Neusner, in *Judaism,* Vol. 19, No. 3, Summer, 1970, © 1970 by American Jewish Congress; Jewish Publication Society and American Jewish Committee for Lou H. Silberman, "Concerning Jewish Theology in North America: Some Notes on a Decade," in *American Jewish Yearbook,* Vol. 70, © 1969 by Jewish Publication Society and American Jewish Committee; Theodore Herzl Foundation and Arthur A. Cohen for "Between Two Traditions," by Arthur A. Cohen, in *Midstream,* Vol. 12, No. 6, June–July, 1966, © 1966 by Theodore Herzl Foundation; American Academy of Political and Social Science for "Jewish Theology Faces the 1970's," by Eugene B. Borowitz, in *Annals of the American Academy of Political and Social Science,* Vol. 387, January, 1970, © 1970 by American Academy of Political and Social Science; Jewish Liberation Project and Dr. Judah J. Shapiro for "The Philistine Philanthropists," by Judah J. Shapiro, in Jewish Liberation Journal, Vol. 1, No. 4, October, 1969, © 1969 by Jewish Liberation Project.

CONTENTS

AMERICAN JUDAISM
Adventure in Modernity

INTRODUCTION

WHAT HAPPENS TO RELIGIOUS TRADITIONS in modern times? Historians describe the development of institutions and doctrines, while sociologists uncover their social foundations. Historians of religions, however, tend to concentrate attention on archaic, or pre-modern, religious life, particularly in the Far East, Africa, South Asia, and the Middle East. They have developed questions about the nature of archaic religions and provided illuminating perspectives. Here we shall ask the questions of historians of religions about people heretofore neglected by them: religious men in modern America. The data differ from all others studied by historians of religions because they derive from a secular, modern, technologically advanced and intellectually sophisticated civilization. And that is why for the study of the history of religions, America, with the contemporary West it represents, is a new and unexplored field of inquiry.

If we were anthropologists studying the religion of a pre-literate tribe, we should ask about the rituals and myths of that tribe, the character of its religious leadership, the social structures that embody its religious traditions, the way in which individual identity is defined. So too of America. We want to know about the religious rituals, beliefs, and stories that shape people's minds, the religious leaders and their place in those beliefs and stories, the religious institutions, the role of religion in the larger society. But with this difference: America is no tribe, but a complex and heterogeneous society. Americans are not pre-literate, but in their masses highly educated. Religiosity in skeptical, modern America is a different sort of thing from the believing in an archaic society that takes for granted the central propositions of religion, as of the broader culture, and knows nothing of doubt or unbelief.

What does it mean to be religious in America? The question is too abstract, the data insufficiently digested. Here, we focus on a small part of that question, on a group that is both well-documented and intensely self-concerned, the Jews. They form a coherent group in American society. They generally regard their group as religious, though doing so requires the revision of commonplace definitions of religion. And their intellectuals have articulately addressed themselves to what it means to be a Jew in America.

Still more interesting, the Jews came from a society that stood on the threshhold of modernity to a country that had long before become its bastion. Central and Eastern European Jewry, which supplied the vast majority of emigrants to America, had experienced no Renaissance to focus attention on man and his achievements; no Reformation to revise the traditional religion and to purify and articulate its doctrines; no Enlightenment to impose on the tradition the astringent criteria of reason and rationality; no Romantic recovery of tradition in a post-Enlightenment reaction; and no Darwinian age of Progress. The five formative centuries of Western civilization passed unnoticed, with little effect, over Central and Eastern European Jews. They came from agricultural villages to the American metropolis, from traditional patterns of human relationships to impersonal ones, from a primitive to a highly developed economic system, from a society where the stranger was an outsider to one in which all were alien to one another, from an intensely religious to a secular world. These changes produced a vast transformation of their religious life, and that is the problem of our study: What has happened to Judaism, and what does it mean to be a Jew today?

The answer to that question does not lie in the study of the history and sociology of American Jewry, or even of American Judaism. We are not going to rehearse the oft-told tales of how in 1654 a few Jewish families came to New Amsterdam, or of the three "waves" of immigration, Spanish, German, and Russian, or of the role of the Jews in fighting for America, or of the founding of various synagogues and national religious movements. Among the several good introductory studies of American Jews and Judaism, Nathan Glazer's *American Judaism* is outstanding.[1] But all that

---

[1] Nathan Glazer, *American Judaism* (Chicago: University of Chicago Press, 1957). From THE CHICAGO HISTORY OF AMERICAN CIVILIZATION, Daniel J. Boorstein, ed.

is needed to answer our question lies in the pages of this book, though many works not quoted here deepen and broaden the inquiry. On the whole, such works concentrate on outward things: the place of Jews in American society and culture; the development of their institutions, synagogues, and community organizations; the way in which Jews became Americans. These issues dominated the interest of scholars for whom what it meant to be a Jew was generally clear and readily defined. What was problematical was the way in which Jews fit into the larger picture of American life.

Today Jews are sufficiently well integrated into that picture so that one need not wonder whether and how a well-defined foreign body is to be assimilated into a stable and equally well-defined social and cultural structure. After four generations, to be Jewish is a mode of being an American, taken for granted by Jews among other Americans, and no longer problematical. The dominant patterns and institutions of American Jewry have been established for nearly a century. What now remains to be explored is, What do Jews now do because they are Jewish? What do they think, how do they respond, when they do as Jews, to the issues of human existence in America? What has happened to their religious tradition—the whole of it, not merely the theological surface? What of the inner life of people who superficially are the most modern of men? Nathan Glazer observes in "The Jews":

> A leading figure in Jewish community affairs relates that a Jew always eagerly asks, in any situation, "How many are Jews?" And when he gets an answer, he asks suspiciously, "How do you know?" Self-consciousness, curiosity, pride—all these are Jewish traits; caution, timidity, fear—these are Jewish traits, too.[2]

The search for "Jewish traits" is not our task. What we want to know is much less than, "Who are the Jews?" or "What is a Jew?" We merely ask, "What is the state of 'Judaism' in contemporary America?" Defining "Judaism" as the sum of the beliefs and rites described by Jews as the way they are religious, and defining religion as the sum of beliefs and rites through which people explain and shape behavior in relationship to the supernatural or to matters of ultimate concern, we ask, "What does it mean to be a Jew, a protagonist of 'Judaism' viewed as a 'religion'?"

Since the vast majority of professing Jews in America are descended from Eastern European immigrants, we begin with a brief description of the religious setting in which they originated.

---

[2] Nathan Glazer, and Daniel Patrick Moynihan, "The Jews," *Beyond the Melting Pot* (Cambridge, Mass.: MIT Press, 1964), p. 137.

In "The Shtetl Way of Life" Elias Tcherikower states:

> Jews were not regarded, nor did they regard themselves, as Russians or Poles who differed only in religion and occupational concentration from the majority population. In a census of 1772, individuals were classified as "merchants, artisans, laborers, or Jews." Jews constituted an autonomous, isolated, self-enclosed, and collectively responsible social entity. The goings-on in the outside world certainly impinged upon the Jewish community, but were regarded as being of the same order as natural events; most often, as natural catastrophes. There was, relatively speaking, little social interaction that mattered between Jew and non-Jew. What was of significance was what went on in the Jewish world, in the world of the *shtetl*.
>
> *Shtetl* literally means small city. It conjures up, however, an entire way of life. This way of life was all the more intense and pervasive for lack of a "state organization" which could facilitate the desire to "preserve a distinct and unique cultural life ... [and] resist the destructive action of the oppressing states," as has been said with reference to divided Poland. Having faced this problem for centuries and, moreover, without a territorial base, Jews had evolved a distinctive complex of values and institutions. These were all integrated into a religion, a term which is perhaps too narrow to describe the all-encompassing *shtetl* culture. ...
>
> Above all, the *shtetl* was a community of rigid religious orthodoxy. From the moment of waking to the moment of falling asleep, literally scores of individual actions and patterns of behavior were controlled by explicit prescription and proscription. The control, however, came from within: the Jewish child, becoming a man at the age of thirteen, knew full well how to live as a good Jew.
>
> The *shtetl* Jew's frame of reference was the Jewish community. Outside was the world of the *goy,* the alien. While friendly feelings might arise from propinquity and economic interaction, the underlying emotion of Jew toward peasant or landowner was one of mistrust. Hatred and fear were particularly directed toward the representative of government authority. . . . There was, indeed, a great deal of autonomy, the entire area of local civil control being left to the Jewish community. The world of Gentile authority was to be avoided where possible; where contact was inevitable, circumvention, propitiation, or bowing one's head till the storm had passed were the traditional responses. Hostility from without was a constant expectation, though violent outbreaks might be shortlived and few and far between. It followed that loyalty to this hostile, alien world was nonexistent. Similarly absent from *shtetl* thinking was the notion that the Jew might control or manipulate this world.
>
> While Gentiles were not relegated beyond the pale of humankind, the significant human relations were those of Jew to Jew. The

shtetl was regarded from without and from within as a collective. Jews were mutually responsible to one another. Though the individual family functioned as an economic unit, and status differentials were not unknown, in the last analysis there were no rigid vertical distinctions within the Jewish community. Low economic standards compelled some degree of competition, but disregard of others was never carried to the point of deprivation of livelihood. Overshadowing the entire economic picture was the ultimate responsibility of the community for the survival of its members. This placed a limit on the permitted degree of competition and exploitation. Thus the conception of human relations, sanctioned by the religious philosophy underlying the culture, was one of mutual interdependence.

Jews are known as the "People of the Book." The *shtetl* literacy rate was extremely high. Its law was written, formalized. Yet within the extremes of what was explicitly prescribed and what was proscribed by the Torah, the Law, there existed a wide range of behavior, subject to the close scrutiny of public opinion. What *mentshn* (people) would think and say was of cardinal importance. Public opinion, personal, informal pressures, with the weapons of gossip, ridicule, and public shame, were major determinants of one's behavior. They took the place of a police force in seeing to it that the Law was enforced. When these proved inadequate, the forces of boycott, ostracism, and, ultimately, of excommunication could be leveled against the deviant. Thus, in a community with little anonymity, the pressures for conformity were powerful. . . .

Distress was handled through both formal and informal channels. The principle of social justice of the *shtetl* required that its poor, sick, aged, or infirm be cared for. The overall institution responsible for such community services was the *kehila* (the community). The *kehila* maintained orphanages, old-age homes, and schools for orphans or children of parents who could not afford tuition, in those towns large enough to warrant such. Sections of the *hehila* dealt with burials and free loans, provided dowries for needy brides and Passover supplies and clothes for the poor, took care of strangers in the community and assigned people to stay up with the sick. In the larger towns some of these functions were assumed by *hevrot* (societies) independent of the *kehila*. Frequently such *hevrot* were affiliated with a synagogue constituted by men in one occupation (draymen, tailors, and so forth). One of the major duties borne by the relatively well-to-do was to belong to these *hevrot*, or to participate in the activities of one of the sections of the *kehila*. Such affiliation was, moreover, one of the chief avenues to prestige. Recipients of aid were in no way beholden to the donors; it was their due: The word for benefice—*zdaka*—derives from the word for justice. In fact, the donor owed thanks to the recipient for the opportunity to "do a *mizva*" (fulfill a commandment).

Though aid to those in distress was thus dispensed through institutional channels, it was devoid of a formal, impersonal bureaucratic character. Paid personnel was unheard of. Furthermore, assistance was often given directly: The orphan and indigent scholar would "eat days" (get his meals at a different home in the community each day); the beggars would gather at funerals, weddings, and circumcisions, and make their regular rounds on Friday afternoons; the well-to-do housewife would send meat and fish to her poorer sisters for the Sabbath. In sum, it was the duty of Jews to aid brother Jews. In the alleviation of distress the Jewish community was, at it were, an extended family. This was the ideal and, in large measure, the reality.

No matter how explicit the folkways of a community, life constantly poses situations which require interpretation and application of the traditional rules. Moreover, some people invariably have more power than others. The criteria in the *shtetl* for occupying positions of leadership, influence, and decision-making were three: scholarship, wealth, and *yihus* (prestige), the latter being an intangible virtue associated with fine families of unquestionable morality and good deeds, living a refined, genteel life. The three often, though not invariably, went together. Wealth provided the leisure for study, an intellectual prodigy could often marry into a wealthy family of *yihus*. The rabbi of the community was its leader only if there was none other who took precedence over him in scholarship and in *yihus*. Leadership, however, had to be constantly validated by proof of one's learning and by good deeds. This was no easy task, for the eyes of the community were always on one. Wealth in and of itself was subsidiary to the possibility it allowed for study, gentility, and good deeds. *Lomdes* (scholarship), on the other hand, had inherent virtue. Since all Jews but the worst boors partook of scholarship to some extent, the world of the mind was familiar to all but a few, and the intellectual leaders of the community were not immune to criticism or surveillance. Authority and leadership were indisputably important, and an element of submissive, charismatic obedience was present in the relationship of followers to leaders, particularly in the Hasidic congregations. Leadership was far from being democratic. Nonetheless, there were strong elements of rationality, and constant scrutiny, in the position of *shtetl* authorities. . . .

Moving up on the ladder of occupation was eminently desirable and approved by the community. Rank in the *shtetl* was far from being permanently fixed. *Shtetl* culture was, in a sense, pragmatic: All activities were measured on the basis of their efficacy in promotion of scholarship, acquisition of wealth and *yihus*. While pleasure was not taboo, it was always secondary to the ultimate purpose of an activity. The typical *luftmentsh* was always preoccupied with formulating some scheme that would enable him to improve his status. There was a sufficient sense of reality, however, for the poor to focus their dreams of mobility, to rest their hopes, on their children rather than on themselves. If a lad showed the slightest promise, no sacrifice by his parents was too great to give him the best education and opportunities. A family could improve its status in two ways: indirectly, by the successful marriage of a scholarly son into a well-to-do family; and directly, by a stroke of luck, aided by hard work, in business. The wage worker was, therefore, strongly motivated to become a tradesman; the artisan, to concentrate on the commercial aspect of his occupation.

This, then, was the relatively static *shtetl* of the mid-nineteenth century. It was, over and above all, an integrated religious community. The meaningful world for its inhabitants was of and with Jews. The individual *goy* and the authority world of the *goyim* were deeply mistrusted and aroused no loyalty. Jews were collectively responsible for one another. The pressures for conformity, based on an all-embracing Law, were powerful. The community had many mechanisms for expressing the interdependence of its members. It had institutions and channels for resolving conflicts without resorting to outside authority and for alleviating distress. These institutions were personal in nature. Leadership and power in the community were based on scholarship, wealth, and *yihus*. Waking hours in the *shtetl* were working hours, idleness being considered sinful. Study and observance of the Sabbath were of overriding importance. . . .[3]

It would be an error to conclude that the immigrant Jews of the last century were all participants in the *shtetl*-culture and its traditional values. Before the nineteenth century was half over, that culture had begun to change under the impact of the modernization of East European economic and social life. Nathan Glazer refers to the effects of that change.

. . . Figures cannot suggest the intensity of the Judaism of the East European Jews, which not only was unique in world history but represented something of a peak even in Jewish history. The East European Jews were attached to a religion that completely enveloped their lives and dictated a large part of their behavior. . . .

But this was only half the picture of the spiritual life of the East European Jews. For they too had been to some extent affected by contemporary thought, by rational philosophy, modern science, and contemporary radical social movements. In Germany, the effect of the modern world on the Jews had been to lead many to conversion and assimilation and others to create Reform Judaism. In eastern

3 Elias Tcherikower, "The Shtetl Way of Life," in Elias Tcherikower, ed., *The Early Jewish Labor Movement in the United States*, trans. and rev. by Aaron Antonovsky from the original Yiddish (New York: Yivo Institute for Jewish Research, 1961), pp. 5–11 (excerpts).

Europe, its effect was quite different. The East European Jews did not convert in any significant numbers, they did not assimilate, and they did not attempt to transform the traditional religion. The first impact of the Enlightenment, of Western ideas in brief, on the East European Jew led to a movement to create a modernized Hebrew tongue, which could be used for the political and cultural uplift of the masses. In time, the new ideas from the West led to the rise of powerful nationalist (Zionist and non-Zionist) and socialist movements: None of them had any place for religion, traditional or reformed.

It is worth considering why it is that the impact of the Enlightenment on German Jewry created Reform, while the Enlightenment in eastern Europe created radical, antireligious movements. There seem to have been two reasons. For one, traditional Judaism was far stronger in eastern Europe in the late nineteenth century than it had been in Germany in the early years of the century. East European Jewish life was remarkable, even in Jewish history, for the single-mindedness with which it pursued the study of the Jewish law and banned every other form of education as heretical. Everything about the law became holy; even the fact that Yiddish was used to expound the Talmud gave that language a kind of holy character, and it became unthinkable that the Talmud might be expounded in Russian or German or English. No rabbi broke with traditional Judaism to lead or demand something like German Reform in eastern Europe; the prospect would have struck him as so hopeless that he would have decided rather, as many did, to abandon any ideas of religious leadership. In Germany, by contrast, traditional Judaism had already moved by the early nineteenth century some distance from its most extreme forms, and there were not only rabbis to lead reforms but many in the middle group who gave the reformers partial support.

Perhaps more important than this were the differences between German and eastern European society. The Jews of Germany lived in an ethnically homogeneous society which was attempting to become a modern national state. They could envisage themselves becoming a religion, like the Lutherans or Roman Catholics, and enjoying all the benefits of full citizenship and perhaps even social equality; only their peculiar customs, they thought, stood in their way. In eastern Europe, it was impossible to think this way. The countries of eastern Europe were not ethnically homogeneous and religiously diverse as was Germany. They were composed of many national groups, some struggling to free themselves from the oppression of others. Religion tended to be intimately tied up with nationality: the Poles were Catholic; the Russians, Greek Orthodox; the German enclaves, Protestant; and so on. In such a situation, the Jews, and the non-Jews too, naturally thought of the Jews as a nation, for that is what they were in eastern Europe. It was easier to envisage the Jews abandoning their religion and becoming simply a people than to envisage them abandoning their ethnic characteristics and becoming a denomination in Reform Jewish style. East European Jews thought of the problems they faced in *national* terms, and the main point of Reform Judaism, that the Jews were, or would become, a religion, appeared meaningless to them, and indeed, in eastern European terms, it was meaningless. . . .

. . . Socialism, anarchism, Zionism, and other radical secular political movements flourished among the East European Jews, particularly among those who moved to the cities from the small towns. There were Zionist socialists who wanted to set up a socialist state in Palestine; national socialists who wanted socialism with minority rights for the Jews in eastern Europe; and antinational socialists who simply wanted socialism and assumed, following Marx, that the Jews, as a decadent caste of merchants tied to capitalism, would disappear once socialism was established. Then there were Zionists of various persuasions: those who were socialist, those who were religious, those who wanted a Jewish state because it would revive Jewish culture, and those who simply wanted a Jewish state in Israel and did not care about religion one way or another. Then there were the Diaspora nationalists, those who wanted to see the Jews legally established as a separate nation with rights as a minority in Europe. And there were the territorialists who wanted to establish a state anywhere, and there were those who simply wanted to assimilate. Not all these positions were to be found in eastern Europe as early as the 1880's, of course; forty years later they had all appeared in one way or another.[4]

So much for the Jews who came to America three or four generations ago, and who laid the foundations for Jewry today. What of contemporary Jewry? No one supposes they have preserved either the religious intensity or the religious intellectuality of their great-grandfathers. Glazer brings us to our subject, contemporary American Judaism.

What in the feelings and sentiments of Jews can we see as reflecting their ancestral religion?

We must begin with something that has not happened; this negative something is the strongest and, potentially, most significant religious reality among American Jews: it is that the Jews have not stopped being Jews. I do not now speak of the fact that they are sociologically defined as Jews; this is of small significance from the point of view of Jewish religion. I speak rather of the fact that they still *choose* to be Jews, that they do not cast off the yoke or burden of the Jewish heritage. Despite the concreteness of the words "yoke"

[4] Glazer, *American Judaism*, pp. 62–66.

and "burden," what I have in mind is something very abstract. It is not that most Jews in this country submit themselves to the Jewish law; they do not. Nor can they tell you what the Jewish heritage is. But they do know it may demand something of them, and to that demand, insofar as it is brought to them and has any meaning for them, they will not answer No. The significance of the fact that they have not cast off the yoke is that they are prepared to be Jews, though not to be the Jews their grandfathers were. The medieval world is gone and Orthodox Judaism is only a survival (as the anthropologists use the word) so far as the majority of American Jews is concerned. But they are prepared to be some kind of Jews; they are capable of being moved and reached and of transcending the pedestrian life that so many of them live in company with other Americans.

In my view, it is because of this negative characteristic, this refusal to become non-Jews, that we see today a flourishing of Jewish religious institutions. It is true that these institutions do not evoke or engage any deep religious impulses and find their greatest strength in a weak acceptance of the mores of middle-class life. Yet they are successful only because American Jews are ready to be Jews, because they are willing to be inducted into Jewish life.

We see the reality of this readiness in the fact that to every generation of recent times a different part of the Jewish past has become meaningful. At the same time, to be sure, other parts of that tradition, great chunks without which it seemed it must die, were rejected. And yet at no point has everything been rejected at once; a kind of shifting balance has been maintained whereby each generation could relate itself meaningfully to some part of the Jewish past. It has been the course of events that has dictated which part of the Jewish past should become more prominent at any given moment—at one time, and for some Jews, it was philanthropy; at another time, and for other Jews, Zionism or Yiddish-speaking socialism; or, as today, institutional religion. The son of the Reform Jewish philanthropist who gives up the last Jewish connection his father maintained may surprise us by becoming what his father never was, a Zionist. The son of the Yiddish-speaking socialist who abandons his father's movement may join the Reform temple. In this way, each generation shoulders a minimal part of the yoke.

There are even more complex patterns than this in the maintenance of a minimal relation to Judaism. There are American Jews who have been given a good traditional education and who, following the pattern of the twenties or thirties, have broken with all religious observance. They do not attend the synagogue, they do not observe the dietary laws, they do not mark the Jewish holidays, and they do not believe in the existence of God. When this kind of Jew has children, however, he will decide that they should have some sort of Jewish education.

Such a man is not succumbing to suburban middle-class pressures; he can resist them as easily as can the classic village atheist. He may tell himself—and believe—that the children should know what it means to be a Jew, for willy-nilly they will be considered Jews and they must know how to cope with anti-Semitism. But one sees at work here that obscure process whereby a minimal relation to Judaism is established. The mental calculus seems to be as follows: Since I myself have had a good traditional education, I can afford to be an agnostic or an atheist. My child won't get such an education, but he should at least get a taste of the Jewish religion.

Philanthropy, Zionism, Jewish organizational life, attachment to Yiddish, an interest in Hasidism, a love of Hebrew, formal religious affiliation, a liking for Jewish jokes and Jewish food—none of these has, on the surface, any particularly religious meaning. Each of them reflects the concerns of the moment. The Protestant social gospel, the needs of Jews in other parts of the world, varied philosophical movements, a tendency to take pride in one's origins—each finds an echo in American Judaism. It is easy to overlook any common element in the different forms of Judaism of the different generations and see only the reflection of movements in society and thought at large. Yet what binds all these shifting manifestations of Judaism and Jewishness together is the common refusal to throw off the yoke. The refusal to become non-Jews stems from an attitude of mind that seems to be—and indeed in large measure is—a stubborn insistence on remaining a Jew, enhanced by no particularly ennobling idea of what that means. And yet it has the effect of relating American Jews, let them be as ignorant of Judaism as a Hottentot, to a great religious tradition. Thus, the insistence of the Jews on remaining Jews, which may take the religiously indifferent forms of liking Yiddish jokes, supporting Israel, raising money for North African Jews, and preferring certain kinds of food, has a potentially religious meaning. It means that the Jewish religious tradition is not just a subject for scholars but is capable now and then of finding expression in life. And even if it finds no expression in one generation or another, the commitment to remain related to it still exists. Dead in one, two, or three generations, it may come to life in the fourth.

Or, indeed, it may not. Perhaps it is only an act of piety to preserve the relatedness to tradition. Perhaps nothing can come out of it any more, and all that remains for Jews is to act as the custodians of a museum. This is possible, too.

Glazer concludes:

Among other Jews—and this includes Orthodox as well as Conservative and Reform Jews—the problem is the creation of a meaningful Jewish life whose power can make itself felt over those many Jews who remain, and wish to remain, open to the influence of an example. If Judaism is to become in America more than a set of religious institutions supported by a variety of social pressures, it will be by virtue of examples of Jewish lives that in some way are meaningful, that in some way permit one to be a Jew. It would be ridiculous to set up qualifications for these examples, to say that they may spring up in this or that grouping in American Jewish religious life and not in the other. What can fulfill a human life cannot be known in advance. All we can know, from the history of Judaism, is that the abstract demand to seek faith, to find God, tends to find little answer among Jews and that concrete examples of Jewish living must be given before religion has an impact on their lives. Once again, honesty requires one to say that it is likely that no satisfactory example can be given in the modern world, that those moments in Jewish history when the Jews were truly a people of priests and a holy nation required circumstances that can never be repeated.

In the Talmud, the voice of God on occasion interrupts or joins the discussions of the sages. With that customary Jewish circumspectness in speaking of God, it is not, in the text, the voice of God that is heard, rather the echo of the voice . . . for, after the end of the age of prophecy, it was no longer possible to hear the voice of God directly. I have suggested that the Jews are quite a few stages past that. Certainly, they will not hear the voice or the echo, perhaps not even the echo of the echo. But something is still left. What is left is a relation to a tradition in which, from all one can tell, the echo once sounded, and there was a readiness to listen. What can still come of it I do not know.[5]

The East European Jews, whose descendants constitute the greatest part of American Jewry today, thus came right from a traditional society on the verge of breaking up into the modern world. Indeed, the act of migration itself broke the tie of the emigrant to the traditional community. East European rabbis warned that America was not a *kosher* country. Yet their people came to America. In leaving home for an unknown land, the emigrant personally severed the bond that tied himself to the old way of life, and however he might try to recover that old way, it was irrevocably lost. The emigrant not only left, but, by leaving, repudiated the self-contained world of the village. He gave up seeing the stranger as outsider and the homeborn as kinsman, living by the rhythm of the holy calendar, following the daily prayers and rituals of the holy law, accepting the authority of the holy man made holy by his learning, enjoying certainty of who one was, forever hoping for the coming of the Messiah and the return to Zion, and abiding in loyalty to the Torah and studying

5 Glazer, *American Judaism,* pp. 139–42, 148–49.

its teachings. The old way of life was abandoned. But Jews in former ages had left one land for the next, and always had recreated the traditional way of life of the old country. In America some tried, but few succeeded for more than themselves, because the old way of life in the old country had lost its hold, if not upon them, then upon their children. The step into the modern world came not in climbing down the gangplank at Ellis Island, but in climbing onto the carrier that left the *shtetl* for the distant seaport.

The stages of the passage into secular, modern life, from decade to decade and generation to generation, need not detain us. Glazer describes the single predominant characteristic of the present Jew: the choice to remain a Jew. That choice, moreover, carries with it a series of concrete actions and expressions of Jewishness, an ethnic identity, and the larger part of these pertain to Judaism, a religious tradition. What is the character of contemporary Judaism? What do Jews do because they espouse the Judaic religious tradition? What sort of holy men do they look to? How do they understand their own identity as Jews, and what does identification with Judaism mean to them? Why the predominance of Zionism and the centrality of the State of Israel in the consciousness and culture of American Judaism? What has happened to the synagogue, to the study of Torah, to the religious beliefs of Judaism? These are the questions before us. Their answers, in my view, together constitute the Judaic testimony concerning what happens to religious traditions in modern times.

1

HOLY LIFE

IN ARCHAIC JUDAISM THE HOLY LIFE—the things one did to conform to the will of God, or, in secular terms, the behavior patterns imposed by the Judaic tradition—was personal and participative. Every man, woman, and child had a myriad of deeds to do because he was a Jew. No one was exempt from following the holy way of living. Everyone expected to share in it equally. One did not speak of how others should keep the Sabbath. One kept the Sabbath, along with everyone else in the community. Everyone individually said his own prayers, advanced his own education in the tradition, did good deeds on his own part for his fellow man. Prayer, study, and the practice of good deeds were personal and universal. To be a Jew meant to do a hundred *mitzvot,* holy actions, every day.

In modern America, to be a Jew primarily means to join an organization, but not personally to effect its purposes. The individual is lost in the collectivity. Joining means paying dues, providing sufficient funds so that other people may be hired to carry out the purposes of the organization. The "joining" is the opposite of what it means, for it is impersonal and does not bring people together, but verifies their separateness. The relationship of man to man is reduced to the payment of money. It is passive, for one does not actually do much, if anything at all. Universally condemned by the preachers, "checkbook Judaism" is everywhere the norm.

What has happened is that the primary mode of being Jewish—living the "holy life"—has moved from the narrow circle of home, family, and small group to the great arena of public affairs and large institutions. The formation of large organizations, characteristic of modern life, tends to obliterate the effective role of the individual. In the Judaic situation, however, even the synagogue, with its substantial budget and massive membership, its professional leadership and surrogate religiosity, follows the pattern. If to be a Jew now means to take an active part in the "Jewish Community," then the holy life is lived chiefly by paying one's part of the budget of the organizations that call themselves the community.

This is how the late Harold Weisberg describes the consequent intellectual and social patterns.

> Programs, plans, and organizations are precisely what appeal to most American Jews. Not only are their ideological ambitions considerably less demanding than those of the intellectuals and independent theologians; they usually can be fulfilled in an institutional manner. In fact, one of the distinguishing features of community ideologies is their capacity for programmatic translation. The search for community and identity among most American Jews is a very practical undertaking and the genius of the Jewish community is organization. Jewish life in the United States is expressed primarily through a culture of organizations. To be a Jew is to belong to an organization. To manifest Jewish culture is to carry out, individually or collectively, the program of an organization. Of course, there is a perfectly good sense in which this claim is false; there are many less public and less formal individual manifestations of Jewish culture. Nevertheless, the activity which overwhelmingly dominates American Jewish life is organizational and the ways in which most Jews are "Jewish" are the institutional ways of the synagogue, the center, the welfare fund and the service agency.
>
> What is most striking, perhaps, is the identification of neutral organizational tasks with Jewish culture. It is already standard practice to identify attending meetings, raising funds, distributing organizational literature, speaking or listening to speeches and participating in testimonial dinners with what was once called "a Jewish way of life." These activities do not exhaust Jewish life, but they come quite close to it. What distinguishes the Jew from the non-Jew is, increasingly, not a special ethic, religious discipline, or language, but the intensity and pervasiveness of his organizational commitments and activities. That part of Jewish culture which was once expressed in face to face situations, in the home, in the street, or through the medium of a special group language, has largely disappeared and . . . the great religious discipline which in the past permeated every aspect of individual and communal life is missing. At present Jewish culture in the United States is pre-

dominantly what Jews do under the auspices of Jewish organizations.

It won't do to object that the activities which most concern the community are only a continuation and extension of traditional community interests, or that the causes which are served are only contemporary expressions of traditional Jewish values. Of course, they are that, but to argue in this way is to miss the point. Unlike earlier Jewish societies, our organizational programs and responsibilities are almost the whole of Jewish culture. In fact, they may well be *the* Jewish culture of the United States. Communal organization and its maintenance have been a central preoccupation of Jews for a very long time in a variety of Jewish communities, but the programs of the organizations and the activities involved in sustaining them did not previously suffice for or pre-empt Jewish culture.

A number of factors have contributed to the development of the culture of organizations: the "coming of age" of the American Jewish community and the increased welfare and community institutional apparatus it has required; the enormous burden of overseas responsibilities undertaken by American Jews and the organizational machinery which has been developed to do the job; the striking growth of religious institutions and organizations; and the changed social status of most American Jews. The last point deserves comment here because it has influenced the structure and style of the organizations created by the developments just noted, and also because it has provided some interesting ideological ramifications which have helped justify the culture of organizations.

American Jews reflect the general social and economic changes since the war and possess strikingly similar institutional apparatus and ideological attitudes to those of the general American leisure-consumption-status class. They manifest so many of the traits which sociologists and social critics attribute to the new American bourgeoisie (the familiar "affluent society") that they may be said to epitomize it. But, for our purposes we need emphasize only one aspect of this development—the emergence of new Jewish communities. A large number of American Jews, enjoying considerable leisure time and on the whole something very close to affluence, have moved out of the urban centers in which pre-war Jewry largely resided to a variety of suburbs, some no more than mediocre mass "developments," others quite substantial and "residential." In these new communities they have had to create organizations and community apparatus where none existed before. Many Jews of the large urban centers never before thought about communal organizations like schools, centers, synagogues and welfare agencies. In the pre-war urban centers such apparatus, if recognized at all, was identified with the culturally reactionary immigrant generation. It was just there and was usually regarded with disdain by those who were seeking greater assimilation into the general American community.

Some Ideological Consequences
of the Culture of Organizations

The ideological presuppositions and consequences of this culture may now be sketched.

(1) Caring for the organization and living through it becomes, as we have already observed, the culture of the Jews. It also produces ideologies which seek to justify this pattern of behavior. Primarily, they take two interrelated forms. The first promotes identity with the established community and sanctions the activity of the community as essential to group survival. So much is at stake in the established community organizations that one is obliged to feel loyalty and to commit himself to the destiny of the community. The second suggests that the programs of particular organizations are indispensable to achieving the group purpose, and consequently they must also be encouraged and supported.

(2) This means, in effect, that the various and presumably compatible organizational programs constitute the ideologies of the community. The justification of Jewish identity and involvement in the community often, perhaps too often, consists of a recital of organizational and communal programs, which in turn appear to require no further justification. The "character" of the community is the program of its organizations. And it is this which directly leads to the identification of organizational tasks and responsibilties with "the Jewish way of life."

(3) Another consequence is that the organization and its program reduce and often eliminate the need for individual ideological concern. The organization provides an ideology which one may assume when he joins it. (And let us recall here that one cannot join *the* Jewish community in the United States, only the Jewish organizations which function as a quasi-community.) This is neither unique nor necessarily bad. A culture that cannot provide ideology through institutional means and which must depend on constant individual ideological re-evaluations is in serious difficulty. However, in the American Jewish community this has had the effect of stifling criticism and re-evaluation in the community and of producing hostility against those who practice it outside the community.

(4) Also worth mentioning is the increased status of formal identification with the Jewish community . . . what it means is that part of the ideology of Jewish identification may now be justified on grounds of status. It is part of the preferred pattern of American leisure-consumption-status class life to join religious organizations and to be active in the community. . . . Active Jewish communal identification is no longer sneered at. It is very acceptable. In fact, it is a definite status achievement.

(5) What is often overlooked is that the preponderance of organizational activity is surrogate activity. By that I mean that participation in the organization usually involves doing something for others. Many Jewish organizations are purely service organizations. However, even among those which are not, service to others forms a major part of the organizations' purposes. Obviously, this is a commendable orientation, but it has interesting ideological ramifications. If what I argued earlier is substantially correct, namely that Judaism in the United States is what Jews do under the auspices of Jewish organizations, then a good deal of American Judaism is essentially philanthropic. Granted that some organizational service is cultural as well as philanthropic, the fact remains that involvement in the organization encourages what may be called a "philanthropic attitude." And this is precisely what may make it so attractive to many people. This point can be pushed too far. I am not unmindful of what the organizational involvement provides for the member, nor have I forgotten the various other motives for organizational identification mentioned earlier. But this only serves to reinforce the point. The activity of the organization provides satisfaction in doing something for others and this may well be what contemporary Judaism is all about.

(6) This leads to a final observation. All the factors which have repeatedly been mentioned as components of new social and ideological conditions for American Jews since the war coalesce to make Jewish identification and what may be called "Jewish behavior" considerably less demanding than it was a generation or two ago. This is not a perverse nostalgic reflection. Most of the conditions which contributed to the widespread hostility toward Jewish identification and Judaism before the war have disappeared. Religion is socially and intellectually respectable, Jewish culture is not identified with immigrant culture, and most Jews can now economically afford to participate in a community life which is more than socially acceptable. In addition there is so much less that is behaviorally expected of a Jew today. Bilingualism has declined, dietary laws are not observed by the masses, and a rigorous religious discipline is not considered normative. There were major breaks with tradition thirty and forty years ago of course, but not, I suspect, with such an absence of guilt or with the organizational means to substitute communal activity for religious discipline that we have today. Moreover, the intellectual and emotional demands of the culture of organizations are not burdensome. They are precisely what appeals to the leisure-consumption-status orientation of most American Jews. There is no agony, no turmoil, no anguish. Community ideologies, like middle-class life in the United States, seek to overcome doubt through activity and loneliness through organization. *Angst,* despair,

even inconclusiveness, are not part of the ideology of the community.[1]

What does it mean to an individual to participate in the "culture of organizations"? What does he actually do, once he has become a "member"? Do the members formulate the policy of the organizations they constitute and support? Howard Singer describes the organization member, and introduces the problem of the "leader."

> The average American Jew has been content to exercise no more control over the organizations than the typical city-dweller does over his municipal political machine. He has been unaware of what those organizations were saying and doing in his name. He is usually a member not out of persuasion but out of gregariousness, and group insurance and cut-rate travel plans loom larger in his mind than some press release put out by the national office. If he has a complaint, he must remember to submit it to the resolutions committee three months before the convention opens next year. But pay your dues at the end of this meeting, fellas, or you won't be eligible to take part in the lodge bowling championship next Thursday night.
>
> The typical member will not go to chapter meetings. He will be content to mail his check once a year, serenely confident that the organization is "doing something for Jews and Judaism." But the handful of volunteers and professionals at the top have their own axes to grind.
>
> Jewish organizations are eager to speak as the voice of American liberalism, or at least as the leading soloists in the liberal chorus. The American Jewish Congress, for instance, has just gone off to battle that venerable institution, the military chaplaincy, on the grounds that the chaplaincy is a violation of the principle of separation of church and state. Now, the average American Jew can think of a thousand Jewish problems that are more pressing. No Jewish interests are involved. The fact that rabbis in uniform, like priests and ministers, are paid by the American government bothers only the lockstep, doctrinaire leadership of the American Jewish Congress. But Americans are sentimental about the chaplaincy, and by attacking it, the American Jewish Congress leadership committed the Jewish community to a destructive conflict Jews could well avoid.
>
> What makes them do things like that?
>
> Part of the answer is that the ambitious men who get to the top of such organizations are often less interested in Jews than in doing a pirouette on the larger national stage. They are essentially liberal theoreticians who use the Jewish organizations as their power base,

---

[1] Harold Weisberg, "Ideologies of American Jews," in Oscar I. Janowsky, ed., *The American Jew: A Reappraisal* (Philadelphia: Jewish Publication Society, 1964), pp. 347–53.

their captive constituency. That's why they utter pronunciamentos on general political issues. That's why the American Jewish Congress behaves as if it were under the delusion that it is really the American Civil Liberties Union. Well, it isn't. Neither is it the conscience of the American people, nor even of American Jewry. It is a small secular organization established to protect the interests of the Jewish people. But long ago it "graduated" and went looking for new worlds to conquer. It didn't conquer any, but it hasn't gone back to its primary function either. All it really has to do is produce a steady stream of press releases. Like most other Jewish organizations, its success is measured not by solid accomplishment but by the column inches it gets in the *New York Times*. The American Jewish Congress may be neither a congress, nor typically American, nor especially Jewish, but in all fairness, the pattern it presents is no worse than that made by most major Jewish organizations. . . .

One problem is that the Jews who control the Jewish organizations cannot get any headlines out of helping their own people. There is no prestige in it, no cachet. The only way to sell such a program to wealthy liberal Jews who allocate the funds is to convince them that relocating poor Jews would help to improve relations with the blacks.

Jewish organizations see Jews as the group from which funds must be raised, and non-Jews as the group that must be influenced. The organizations try to exert influence in the style of a tenderfoot in an old-time western saloon: They speak softly, they are prepared to ignore some nasty looks, and they are eager to buy drinks for everybody in the hope of making as many friends as they can. But friendship is not won that way. Jews in the United States are a tiny minority, far too weak to affect the broader currents in our society. . . .[2]

The single most important Jewish organization in any community, measured by the sum of the funds it raises and disburses, the numbers of people regularly and actively involved in its program, and the participation of upper-class leadership in its affairs, is the Jewish welfare fund or federation. A ubiquitous phenomenon, the welfare fund began as a joint fund-raising effort of local Jewish charities, starting in Boston in 1895, and spread everywhere as a Jewish community chest. With the rise of America to world power, American Jewry likewise assumed international responsibilities toward persecuted Jews in other places before and after World War II, then toward the establishment and development of the State of Israel after 1948. Those responsibilities could be carried out only through collection of immense sums of money. The need to raise funds corresponded neatly to the social pattern of joining and organizing por-

2 Howard Singer, *Bring Forth the Mighty Men* (New York: Funk and Wagnalls Inc., 1969), pp. 222–24.

trayed by Weisberg and Singer—indeed, gave purpose and meaning to otherwise banal and pointless busy-work.

At the same time, the mobilization of the "community" in annual drives, with captains, lieutenants, and divisions and brigades, medals, prizes, and awards, had its impact upon the quality and character of the "holy life." For one thing, as we shall see, sheer need made wealth the predominant criterion for Jewish leadership. This brought to the fore a new class of holy men, to replace the class, in the old synagogue, of those who were learned in the Jewish traditions. For another, the existing tendencies to reduce ordinary people to "members" and to remove them from the decision-making processes were reenforced. Third, the new class of leaders proved hostile to the separateness, the group life, of the Jews as a community, to the things that make Jews Jewish according to the norms of American society and Judaic tradition. Kenneth Roseman explains the impact of the "culture of organizations" upon the structure of the Jewish community.

> How does one enter the power elite? It appears that there are two ways of entering the power structure: vertically or horizontally. The most common way is vertical mobility, so that a young man begins his career of community service in fundraising, then assumes a committee or board assignment, progresses to the presidency of an individual agency, and finally achieves a top position in one of the central organizations. It is at this last stage that the individual either achieves permanent power or falls out of favor. As Jennings states, "In most organized endeavors, there is a series of steps that those at the apexes have traveled, barring lateral introduction. . . . In non-profit organizations, the process is popularly known as 'going through the chairs.'"
>
> Horizontal mobility, on the other hand, means entering the power structure near the top without "going through the chairs." Because this is not the "normal" way of entering the power structure, it is usually reserved for several special types of individuals. There are, of course, high-prestige persons who can be used for publicity, but it must be remarked: these people do not achieve bona fide power; they remain subservient to the desires of the true members of the power structure. The second type of individual who achieves power by horizontal mobility is the large or potentially large donor who feels that power and prestige are due him by virtue of his money. Finally, horizontal mobility may be used to induce an older man who has money, prestige, and capability to become active in community work. Such an individual cannot, obviously, be asked to start at the lowest levels; he must begin nearer the top.
>
> Not every job in the Jewish community is open to the horizontally mobile individual. Generally, this type of appointment is limited to the top jobs of individual agencies or to second-level

positions in the central bodies, although very infrequently it may be used for the top positions. Since such appointments are resented bitterly by those who have entered the power structure vertically, they are used sparingly and only when the desired results cannot be otherwise achieved. The leaders of the power structure are also somewhat wary about appointing someone to a top position without previously testing him on jobs of lesser responsibility. The horizontally mobile individual is often an unknown quantity.

Regardless of which method of entry an individual uses, he must have certain personal qualities which legitimize his power. Analyzing what qualities or attributes are necessary to achieve lasting power, we found two partially conflicting hypotheses. Although neither is correct in all respects, we tend to agree that the latter is more nearly representative of the way in which the men currently at the top of the power structure achieved their power.

The "democratic view" presumes that any young man can achieve a position of top power if he works hard and successfully, gives generously within his means, and is reasonably "presentable" and well-liked by the power structure. Our research would tend to confirm this idealistic, egalitarian hypothesis to a certain extent. We are convinced that anyone can rise, for example, to membership on the board of an individual agency or even to the board of the central organizations, provided he follows the pattern outlined above.

On the other hand, although our research indicates that personal effort and generosity may secure a measure of power, the conclusion is inescapable that money, family tradition, and a number of similar factors are usually more influential in the final analysis. In our study, we discovered that, of the funds raised during a recent Jewish welfare fund campaign, 60.4 per cent of the money was donated by only 3.7 per cent of the donors. Quite obviously, this places the larger giver in a highly strategic power position. And, as the need for additional funds increases in Jewish community enterprises, one may expect to see an increased concentration of power in the hands of the very wealthy whose gifts alone will determine the success or failure of many communal projects.

Leaders from the Periphery

Typically, the leadership of the power structure is lax concerning Judaism and Jewishness. A historical note is valuable here. Before 1880, Jews of the upper classes appeared to be very secure. There was no excessive need to assimilate, as they were well-accepted by the "Protestant Establishment." By the 1910's, however, mass immigration of Jews and Catholics had occurred in many areas of the country. The direct effect of this immigration was a change in the status for the Jews, for now the immigrants

were seen by the "Establishment" as a potential threat to its political and social power. As a consequence, there appeared a
systematic program of exclusion and discrimination. In this situation, the upper-class Jews were faced with a clear choice. Either
they could seek entry into Christian society, by open conversion
or by merely avoiding anything Jewish, or they could retreat to
the Jewish community and there develop the power and prestige
denied them in the general community. With a few exceptions,
the Jews chose the latter alternative.

Since this time, the position of the Jew in American society has
improved, although he still encounters social exclusion from certain circles. There is a renewed feeling of security among the
leaders. They are more comfortable with their Judaism, as long
as it is minimal and does not interfere with their "more important
concerns." In general, they tend to be observant of only the few
"required practices," such as temple membership and holyday synagogue attendance. While determined to combat anti-Semitism, they
are at pains to carry on the battle without publicity, fanfare, or
exposure of the fact that they still feel marginal enough to be
threatened by anti-Semitic attacks. The "sha-sha" policy is also
predicated upon the belief that more can be accomplished by
informal and behind-the-scenes efforts than by public demonstrations and outcry. Almost all of these men are abysmally ignorant
of anything but the most elementary information about Jewish
history, theology, and practice or about the Bible and Hebrew.
This, however, is not seen as a detriment to their leadership or
power, for their community service is based totally on a secular
ethic.

Underlying their activity, we sense, is still the goal of achieving
prominence in the general community. Consequently, they may
be what Kurt Lewin calls "leaders from the periphery." As he puts
it:

> In any group, those sections are apt to gain leadership which are most
> generally successful. In a minority group, individual members who are
> economically successful, or who have distinguished themselves in their
> professions, usually gain a higher degree of acceptance by the majority
> group. This places them culturally on the periphery of the underprivi-
> leged group and makes them more likely to be "marginal" persons. They
> frequently have a negative balance and are particularly eager to have
> their "good connections" not endangered by too close a contact with
> those sections of the underprivileged group which are not acceptable to
> the majority. Nevertheless, they are frequently called for leadership by
> the underprivileged group because of their status and power. They
> themselves are usually eager to accept the leading role in the minority,
> partly as a substitute for gaining status in the majority, partly because
> such leadership makes it possible for them to have and maintain addi-
> tional contact with the majority.
>
> As a result, we find the rather paradoxical phenomenon of what one
> might call "the leader from the periphery." Instead of having a group

led by people who are proud of the group, who wish to stay in it and to promote it, we see minority leaders who are lukewarm toward the group, who may, under a thin cover of loyalty, be fundamentally eager to leave the group, or who may try to use their power outright for acts of negative chauvinism. Having achieved a relatively satisfactory status among non-Jews, these individuals are chiefly concerned with maintaining the status quo and so try to soft-pedal any action which might arouse the attention of the non-Jewish. [*Kurt Lewin, "The Problem of Minority Leadership," in Alvin W. Gouldner, ed.,* Studies in Leadership *(New York: Harper & Row, Publishers, 1950) p. 193*].

There can be no doubt that presenting a good public image to the non-Jewish community is crucially important to these men. They are in close daily contact with the business, professional, and governmental leaders of the non-Jewish community. No suspicion can be permitted that, in their own Jewish communal sphere, they are unable to maintain control. Consequently, the appearance of harmony and peaceful cooperation must be preserved, even at the expense of sacrificing or compromising principles. The leadership also maintains explicitly that a good public image is necessary to the fulfillment of its goals within the Jewish community. Even so, preserving a good image is not the entire explanation for the insistence on communal harmony. Even apart from the public relations problem, the top men in the power structure are committed to the idea that, at all costs, the organizational structure must function smoothly and with as few disruptions as possible, and there is a pragmatic basis for this. A disgruntled group within the Jewish community might not contribute to the welfare fund campaign. Funds being at a premium, it is extremely important that no group be alienated so completely that it withdraws or threatens to withdraw its donations. As a result, it is *sh'lom bayis,* communal peace, which has become the cardinal virtue in community operation, often at the cost of fundamental and necessary social planning.

Power and the Professional

The high standards and capabilities of Jewish communal agencies must, in large measure, reflect the high caliber of their professional executives. The current professional leaders of the Jewish community continue to manifest the same elevated competency which marked their predecessors. While there may be individual deviations, the modern professional is technically well-trained and able to operate programs well above the level of comparable programs outside the Jewish community.

One observes, however, that there has been a considerable and growing antagonism between the religious and the philanthropic centers of Judaism. Each of these structures is attempting to gain preeminent power and prestige at the expense of the other. In this competitive situation, the professionals appear to have elected a policy of militant secularism—making as few concessions as possible to Jewishness. The feeling among the professional executives seems to be that for them to identify themselves with overt Jewishness would somehow constitute both a defeat at the hands of the temple or synagogue and a dilution of their professional standards. It might be noted, in passing, that the tide of battle has been uniformly in favor of the philanthropic structure—to the extent that religious institutions are now threatened with the very real possibility of becoming vestigial.

There is sustained pressure, however, on the part of the laymen, who insist that community agencies must openly manifest their attachment to Jewish practices and ideals if they are to continue receiving support from the Jewish community. One report advocated "a need for greater Jewish commitment among Jewish social work professionals. . . . Jewish institutions need to clarify their roles in the perpetuation of Jewish group life."

It is this writer's observation that the power of the Jewish community professional is growing considerably. There appear to be several reasons for this development. In the first place, the increasing complexity and specialization of modern communal service mean that the average layman cannot attain the same understanding of agency problems and needs as he formerly could. Inevitably, then, he must place more reliance upon the testimony of the expert, in this case, the professional agency executive.

The importance of the trend must not be minimized. As the layman comes to rely more heavily on the advice of the professional, the power of the latter is extensively broadened, and this applies in particular to policy formation and planning. As a general rule, we may assert that the effective limits on the professional's power are now determined only by his ability or inability to present information which would justify his recommendations and to withhold data which would controvert his plans.

The power of the professional executive in the Jewish community is further increased by another factor which is not altogether unconnected with the first. This is the matter of board member selection and tenure. As the demands of specialization increase, the ability of the layman to contradict the professional decreases proportionately. The professional who wishes to establish a firm basis for his power must recognize this fact and the inevitable conclusions which derive from it. Thus, it is obvious that, in the selection of board members, the professional will be careful to handpick for nomination those individuals who are interested in the work of the agency, but who are neither powerful, aggressive, nor too-well informed. These persons can be "educated" along the lines which the professional chooses. They must also, if possible, be connected with interests whose favor the professional wishes to cultivate. The professional, by so structuring his board, may preserve his expertise and, consequently, his power. Needless to say, this tactic is not always successful. Lay nominating committees have shown themselves determined to preserve at least a measure of independent judgment. Parenthetically, it is to be noted that laymen use different criteria in nominating individuals for board membership. To them, social acceptability, friendship, wealth, and interest are more important.

Another fairly recent development has, paradoxically, helped to secure the power of the professional. In an effort to be more democratic, some boards have limited the terms, both of membership and of office, to approximately four years. The supposed consequence of this was to have been a more representative membership and the advantage of a variety of different opinions. It was also held that, by demanding a turnover in board membership, new people could be involved in agency work, and good workers could be rewarded. Above all, the specter of the "self-perpetuating board" would be banished from communal life.

The effect of this policy has been somewhat unexpected. Before the democratic system was instituted, boards were frequently self-perpetuating; members had life tenure, even permanent occupancy of specific offices. Under this system, it was possible for the individual layman to develop knowledge and expertise enough to act as an effective check on the professional. Now that tenure on boards is limited, the layman is denied this possibility. As soon as he begins to develop a depth understanding of the nature, functions, and problems of an organization, he is forced to leave his office and, on occasion, the board. In practice, this means that the checks on the professional are considerably diluted and that, as a consequence, his power is enhanced.

Still, it must be noted that the professionals in the Jewish community have not taken advantage of the far-reaching potential of power-seeking and empire-building. In general, they have worked closely with the laymen and have shown themselves dedicated to the highest professional standards. They have consistently placed institutional and program success above their personal advantage, although, as is obvious, the two may be tightly intertwined.[3]

Roseman's stress upon the role of the professional leads us to wonder, what do professional Jews, the community fund administrators and the executives of national and local Jewish institutions and organizations, actually want to accomplish? What is the purpose of the Jewish professional who today is arbiter of the holy way? What is his measure of success, both personal and institutional? And what is the impact of the professional Jew upon the formation and realization of the holy way? Judah J. Shapiro describes the inner life of the Jewish welfare fund.

[3] Kenneth D. Roseman, "Power in a Midwestern Jewish Community," *American Jewish Archives*, XXI, No. 1 (April, 1969), 64–66, 72–74, 78–81.

In the spirit of the modern sociology, we should shift our vantage point from considering the poor who are served, to an examination of who is on top. This will lead to the fruitful approach whereby we can understand the Jewish community by knowing the nature and distribution of power in its midst. It is within the Federations that we discover the *top* of the Jewish community.

Beautiful and innocent people are the mainstay of these Federations, making contributions to their annual campaign for funds in the conviction that their support is their tangible identification with fellow Jews in need of financial assistance at home and abroad. This annual pledge and its payment is the modern equivalent of being a card-carrying Jew. Theology, ideology, value-systems, and ritual are all secondary to the support of the Jewish Federation and Welfare Fund as evidence of one's Jewishness.

In these circumstances, the innocence of the contributors is the gelatinous culture in which the germs of the power disease incubate and grow. It is not unlike the fallacy of "people's capitalism" whereby widely scattered ownership of industry gives power to a managerial class, undreamed of in the days when one really had to own a business with one's own money to exercise so much power over others. So, in the realm of Jewish philanthropy today, largely centralized by Jewish Federations and Welfare Funds, power is the province of those who manage the contributed funds of the numerous well-intentioned individuals who provide their money as an expression of Jewish solidarity and concern for fellow-Jews.

The new role of the Federations during these past twenty-five years has produced many new problems, mainly pertaining to the way in which the local Jewish Federations function as the final and ultimate arbiters of Jewish communal affairs. A distinguished record of fund-raising in dire circumstances for European Jewry and in support of the risen State of Israel has unfortunately made obscure the pressing issue of Jewish communal viability in this country and the need for the participation of individuals other than .the rich, as well as the requirement of this society for a community which permits democratic participation of its constituents, makes leadership accountable to its adherents, and provides opportunities for dealing with aspirations of the group as well as urgencies of welfare clients.

In a comparison with industry, the Jewish Federations come out a poor second, even with respect to the superficial aspects of democratic procedures. By law, shareholders in industry have opportunities to vote on policy and administrative matters, at least by proxy. In Jewish Federations there is no election in which the shareholders have a voice with respect to the selection of leadership, the approval of policy, or the choice of alternatives. There is not even a poll of sentiment with respect to actions taken.

This means, in fact, that there is no accountability of the leadership to the contributors, to the Federation's constituency. It is sometimes difficult to believe that these Federations function in the U.S., where no undertaking by the leadership of a union, for example, has validity without the vote of the union's membership, as a matter of law; and where a variety of public opinion polls are constantly assessing the satisfaction of the electorate with the performance of elected officials.

There is an explanation of the studied avoidance of hearing the voice of the people. It is too obvious that the goals of the people and of Federation leadership are by now far apart, and being a *voluntary association,* the leadership would not long support a program other than its own, even if the program were that of the majority of the people. The *leadership,* therefore, is really without a following, nor does the Jewish population of any locality really have an organized community recognizable by any of the usual definitions of social and political science.

Until the later 1930's the Federations were the limited instrument for maintaining the charitable enterprises, mainly in the health and welfare category. They had no awareness and little concern for the Jewish community as an entity with common aspirations among its individual adherents, involving such matters as cultural identity, Jewish education, ideological positions, and political viability. The annual campaign of the Federation was generally in support of the sick and the poor, and later, the psychologically disoriented. Other and separate campaigns pursued the goals of overseas relief, Zionism and its quest for establishment of a Jewish State, education and cultural institutions, and political movements. The overseas events and their consequences required financing and it was generally conceded that the greatest hope for maximum financial support was the centralization of all Jewish fund-raising.

No one should detract in any way from the value of the massive assistance which was provided by the high-powered campaigning within the context of Federations and Welfare Funds. The questions to be considered and acted upon are the methods and processes for the disposition of the funds.

There is, first, a basic question about the appropriateness and competence of welfare-oriented personalities to deal with educational and cultural matters. As one social scientist has expressed it: "The policy conclusions that can be reached by a factual analysis of the problems of education are not as specific and indisputable as those arrived at by surveying the current health situation in the light of modern knowledge." Yet in Jewish Federations, the *ad hoc* quality of decisions in the health field are imposed upon programs whose implications are long-term and of generational significance.

There are also deeper aspects of the new definition of the

Federations' communal roles. The managerial class is best defined by the title of a recent volume on the social work profession, *The Professional Altruists*. It is in itself a commentary on our society that "having regard for others," which is the dictionary definition of altruism, is a profession. But in the complexities of modern society one must discard the nineteenth-century abhorrence of bureaucracy and accept that we must be bureaucratic. The real question is whether we have good or bad bureaucrats.

In the Jewish Federations, the test of a good executive is his contribution to the raising of funds, rather than his identification with group aspirations. One listens to a new language, by which an executive claims the distinction of having gone "from three point eight to four point two." This means that his claim to fame is that the city where he worked has advanced from raising $3,-800,000 to the sum of $4,200,000 during this executive's incumbency. This is so good a record that he becomes eligible for assignment to a larger city where he can start with "five point one" in the expectation that he will be moving toward "six." In the nature of things, this executive is responsible for the bulk of the fund-raising in his city for Israel, but may despise Zionists. He is seen to be the executive of the Jewish communal interests but is himself without Jewish education or prior Jewish identification.

The lay leadership, in contradistinction to the professional altruists, has become the ultimate in amateur egoism. It does not buy itself out of participation in Jewish affairs by making a contribution, as used to be the style of the rich; it makes its contribution with the understanding that it will have a role in the decision-making. Its amateur status in Jewish affairs is a contradiction of the very meaning of modernization in the political science sense, whereby one's status is by achievement rather than by ascription. The recognizable achievements of this laity is in every field—business, law, and government—except the area of Jewish affairs. Entrance into Jewish leadership begins with the size of one's financial support of the Federation, and once there, the criteria of the individual's success in other spheres ascribe to him similar competence in the Jewish field. The Jewish Federation becomes for such individuals a club, exclusive and personal, rather than a communal instrument for the Jews of the locality in their pursuit of group goals.

There are many dilemmas now faced by American Jewry which ought to be matters of public discussion and group decision. Were the Federations democratically constituted, these might be occurring within that context. For example, all Jewish organizations enjoy sending telegrams to the Soviet Union protesting the treatment of Yiddish writers, but a Yiddish writer could starve in the major cities of this country without the same organizations doing anything to alleviate the situation. The protests to the Soviet Union would come with better grace were it possible to say that in the country of the protesters, Yiddish writers have the support of the free Jewish community.

What is one to do, and who is to decide about keeping the Jewish historical record? The Philistine attitude towards Jewish cultural enterprise has several reputable and competent agencies in the direst circumstances. The employees of certain Jewish cultural agencies earn considerably less than these who remove the garbage from the streets of New York City. Newspapers, letters, and books of the greatest historical value, at least for those who may later compose the history of earlier periods, are inadequately protected and their accessibility is limited. Efforts are afoot to get the project for the Great Yiddish Dictionary out of this country and to Israel to assure its ultimate completion because there is no recognition here of the value of such a magnum opus in the cultural-intellectual life of the Jews. No major enterprise for updating text materials; for translations from Yiddish, Hebrew and other languages into English; for programs for youth designed to make them competent for leadership participation, no such enterprises get the ear of the Federations except in pious but ineffectual terms.

There really is no leadership in Jewish affairs in this country today, for those that rule justify the existing programs as the ones the givers are ready to support. Leadership is not that element in our community which formulates programs for which money should be given, and then convinces supporters. That is why we have a Jewish chapel at John F. Kennedy Airport which no interpretation of the Jewish tradition or ethos could justify, but those who provided the funds wished to do it for reasons utterly extraneous to Jewish communal needs. That is why health is the number one priority in Jewish affairs in this country, where Jews are citizens and beneficiaries of whatever health protection the country offers.

The Federation answer to the questions about this priority is inevitably—that's what the givers are ready to support. That is why there are over 30,000 volumes on the Civil War in the Library of Congress, but a request for support of a scholarly undertaking on the history of the Jews of Warsaw obtains a Federation response that there is *a* book on this subject already. Examples of Philistinism are too numerous to record here.

The inhibition to reorienting the Jewish Federations in this country is rooted in the fact that everybody gets something and is not ready to forego the pittance. Zionists know that they have no standing within the top leadership of Jewish Federations but accept the reality of the support of Israel by Federations as reason enough for avoiding any conceptual or ideological conflict with them. And so the Jewish Federations are, in fact, the treasury and the budget bureau of a non-existent Jewish community.

The road to change is two-pronged. There is the possibility of asking out loud all the embarrassing questions about the denial of democratic rights to the Jews of every community where a Federation functions. There is the second possibility of undertaking some research, even if by polling, on what the people think is important and comparing that with what the Federations do. There is no question about the gaps, but they should be recorded with precision and they should be publicized.

There are some exceptions to the distortions in Jewish communal affairs as represented by the primacy of the Federations in the support of Jewish causes. Those exceptions are either in the individuals of given communities, lay and professional, who truly exert themselves on behalf of the concept of community against the pressures described here. They should be supported and have the right to expect encouragement from any who undertake the correction of the present situation; and there are the exceptions in particular communities where enough individuals rise to challenge the powers-that-be, and in such instances more consistent programs of challenge must be formulated and implemented. It would all seem worthwhile, for a Jewish communal reality in an American society, undergoing so much change, requires more than ever a democratic policy. And what we have to lose is a Jewish communal future.[4]

We begin our inquiry with the fundamental questions of *power* in American Judaism: What do people actually do because they are Jewish? Why? What are the effects? Who dictates what to do, or not to do?

What people actually do is join organizations. They do so because they have been convinced that that is what "Judaism" expects of them. They think this primarily because of the patterns established, or already imposed, by others. The result is the concentration of power in the hands of the few who actually determine what organizations do. These few are not democratically elected, but generally come up out of an oligarchy of wealthy and influential men. But even these men do not actually effect the work of the community. They raise the funds and allocate them, but local funds are in fact spent by, and chiefly upon the salaries of, the professional bureaucrats trained to do whatever it is that the organizations do. In general their work is to keep the organization alive and prosperous.

What has all this to do with "being Jewish"? Should we not have

---

4 Judah J. Shapiro, "The Philistine Philanthropists: The Power and Shame of Jewish Federations," *Jewish Liberation Journal,* I, No. 4 (October, 1969), 1, 4.

started with an account of what "the Jews believe" or what "Judaism teaches"? Indeed we should, if what Jews believed and what classical Judaism taught decisively shaped the contemporary realities that define what, in everyday life, it means to be a Jew. Since we asked what it means to be a Jew in America, the first thing we wanted to know is: What does a person do because he is a Jew? And the answer is: He joins an organization and gives money. In this respect, what makes a person *Jewish* in American society primarily depends on which organization he joins and to what worthy causes he gives money.

That the "holy way" should have become the "culture of organizations" tells us that modernity has overtaken the Jews. What characterizes group life in modern times is the development of specialists for various tasks, the organization of society for the accomplishment of tasks once performed individually and in an amateur way, the growth of professionalism, the reliance upon large institutions. What modern man gains in greater efficiency and higher levels of competence cannot be given up because of nostalgia for a way of life few now living in a traditional society would want to preserve. But as everyone recognizes, the cost of "progress" is impersonality and depersonalization. The real question is not whether to return to a more primitive way of living, but how to regain the humanity, personality, individual self-respect, and self-reliance necessarily lost on the new way.

Here the question of religiosity must enter: Can the religious life survive its specialization? Are not the central human issues addressed by archaic religion obscured, obliterated by the modern intervention of "professionals," religious virtuosi?

The human condition has not changed from archaic to modern times: People still grow up, love and wed, bear children and raise them, grow old, sicken and die. The successive stages of human life once were marked by stages in the religious way, new responsibilities bestowed by the holy way. Men died with dignity. They found meaning in their labor. They recognized love. They enjoyed public respect, esteem, prestige. These do not seem idealizations of a world we never knew and would not actually want. Today conditions of life have changed, but the human condition endures, frail and tentative, above all transient.

So the task before the modern Jew, as with other modern men, must be the recovery of a human way of living, of a context for the passage of life, and above all, of a coherent mythic setting in which to explore life's private meanings. And the way to that recovery lies through the exploration of what in the archaic situation still retains meaning: So far as men once died and still do, the living may learn from the dead how to die. What is false in the culture of organizations is not its modernity, but its irrelevance to the human condition. What is valid in that culture is its adaptation to contemporary means of achievement of the old, collective effort to secure a decent society.

Let us now digress, to see the place in contemporary American Judaism of the holy man of archaic Judaism, the rabbi. One of the questions facing historians of religions is, after all, not only what is the present state of affairs, but also, how do institutions change in the passage from archaic to secular times. The outstanding figure of archaic Judaism, onetime embodiment of all that is holy, is the rabbi. In the old holy life, he led the way. What is his place in the new?

2

HOLY MAN

THE "PROFESSIONAL JEWS" who run the Jewish institutions and organizations that constitute for the ordinary folk the "holy way" are anonymous,
faceless, wholly secular. People relate to them no differently than they do
to other bureaucrats, in government offices, public schools, department
stores. One Jewish functionary, however, the common people continue to
regard as quintessentially "Jewish," important, and formative of values,
and that is the least powerful and least effective figure, is the rabbi. For
nearly twenty centuries the rabbi was the holy man of Judaic tradition.
He became a rabbi through study of Torah, which comprehended not
only the Hebrew Scriptures, but also the Oral Torah, believed to have
been handed on in Mosaic revelation and eventually recorded in the pages
of the Babylonian Talmud and related literature. The rabbi was a holy
man consecrated not by prayer, though he prayed, nor by asceticism,
though he assumed taxing disciplines, but by study and knowledge of
Torah. That knowledge made him not merely learned or wise, but a saint,
and endowed him with not only information, but also insight into the
workings of the universe. Consequently, in former times rabbis were believed to have more than commonplace merits, therefore more than
ordinary power over the world, and some of them, especially qualified by
learning and piety, were seen able to pray more effectively than common
people and to accomplish miracles. What did the rabbi actually do in

traditional Jewish society? Stuart E. Rosenberg describes the life of the rabbi:

The medieval rabbi was not yet a parish worker; little pastoral visiting was done by him. This function was performed by the laity in general, and in many cases by the lay heads of the community. He still retained his traditional position of teacher and scholar and was, as in earlier times, linked with the school. Nor did the rabbi feel himself attached to any single synagogue in a city possessing more than one. On the Sabbath he would usually worship in the oldest and most respected synagogue of the city. There, he was given a special seat next to the Holy Ark. During the week he seldom visited any synagogue, preferring to pray either at home or in the school with his students, prior to beginning the day's studies.

The rabbi was still not a leader of synagogue ritual, nor was he a liturgical official, as he has become in America. True, he still decided all problems of ritual and liturgy, but he did this as a scholar who was best acquainted with Jewish law and tradition, not in the capacity of a synagogue official. While in the early days of rabbinic professionalization the rabbi did come into closer alignment with the school as its official administrator, he had not yet merged his office with the functions of the synagogue. The medieval synagogue remained a communal institution, controlled in most instances by the law officialdom of the Jewish community.

Still another area of competence and authority occupied the medieval rabbi's special talents: He was the judge of the community. Jewish law prevailed in all countries of the dispersion, and since legal authority was the basis of the *Morenu* diploma, the rabbi was called upon to exercise his powers of interpretation in both civil and religious law. No situation among Jews that required litigation would be brought to a non-Jewish court. Thus, a variety of problems, ranging from the interpersonal to the commercial, were laid before the rabbi for his decision. It was principally as a result of such a condition that the medieval rabbi, in many ways, was still able to retain his pre-eminence as the authoritative religious leader of the community in spite of the fact that he had become a professional civil servant.

The medieval Jewish world had made him into a civil servant-clergyman. But the modern Jewish community would make the rabbi into something even different—the Jewish counterpart of a Protestant minister. The desire for emancipation caused Jews to seek to assimilate non-Jewish thought and institutions into their religious and communal life. But for such hopes and aspirations the medieval rabbi, like the medieval Jewish community, would never do! They may not have been ready to say what kind of a rabbi they really wanted, but the Jewish candidates for emancipation seemed to know very well what kind they did not want. Pointing their fingers at the rabbis they saw around them, their criticism revealed the desire to revamp the style and the structure of their religious institutions, to make them conform to Christian procedures:

> *For the welfare of your community you do nothing; you do not teach them the fundamentals of religion, you do not supervise the education of their children. You preach no moral sermons, you do not visit the sick at heart or prepare the dying for repentance . . . No communal matter ever comes before you; you deal only with the butchers and the cooks, rendering decisions on forbidden foods.*

Never before in Jewish history had the laity expected the rabbi to act as pastor and counselor, nor considered it necessary for the rabbi to be a "preacher." Fundamentals of religion were left to the elementary teachers in the Jewish schools. The rabbi was the judge, the scholar, the academic philosopher, and, in the medieval community, an ecclesiast, serving under the control of the autonomous lay council. Now the spirit of emancipation was sweeping across western Europe, and he was to become something new altogether.

The ancient rabbis were the lay teachers and guides of the total Jewish community. The modern American rabbi has become but a staff member, albeit "chief of staff" of a private Jewish membership club, the synagogue of the twentieth century. He no longer really "belongs" to the whole community, or even to the "whole" synagogue; he is but the paid official of one denominational group, which is often in serious competition with the "other" synagogues: the rival claimants to religious domination. As a competitive staff head, he is expected to offer better and more efficient service to "his" organization than the other staff heads in the community. Indeed, this is the way in which his effectiveness as a rabbi is often measured. Yet as rabbi he knows that Judaism cannot be institutionalized; it is a tradition and a way, not an institution.

That the modern rabbi is expected to emulate the pattern of public behavior of the Christian clergy is so apparent that it needs no elaboration here. But in the very nature of a rabbi's calling and training his tasks are essentially scholarly, not ecclesiastical; pedagogical, not liturgical. He is not ordained in the synagogue or by the synagogue, in order to serve the synagogue, as is the case among Christian religious groups. He is called to serve as a "Rabbi in Israel": a teacher of his people, nothing more, but surely nothing less. The greatest of the Jewish prophets, Moses, is still known as *"Moshe Rabbenu,"* not priest, cleric, or ecclesiast, but "Moses, our Teacher." It is in this role that the modern rabbi is least known, perhaps, because most American Jews are no longer willing students of Judaism. Yet the rabbi knows that if he is not a teacher, he is really not a rabbi.

In historical perspective, too, not only has the rabbinical calling been reshaped, if not reduced, but the territory of the rabbi's concern has been sharply rolled back. In the ancient community, he was teacher and master of all; in the medieval world he slowly came under community rule, was often made into nothing more than a pawn in the hand of the city's bureaucrats; in our time, his boundaries have been further restricted: He is not even a symbol of *the* synagogue, only of *a* synagogue. As a result, he is identified by others, and inevitably has come to idenitfy himself with only part of a community: the religious part. A new dichotomy thus enters American Jewish life, a dichotomy that has its roots in the medieval world of the rabbi—the religious ranged against the nonreligious, the sacred against the secular. More and more, the rabbi has been forced into becoming an official protagonist of the synagogue, as if the synagogue were a thing apart from the community. In the process, he often comes to see the non-synagogue community as nonreligious, as if they were "outsiders." Yet, as a rabbi, he knows that Judaism is not synonymous with church-religion; the spiritual life of Judaism is not coterminous with membership in a synagogue. The thoughtful rabbi knows that even Jewish secularism has roots deeply embedded in the religious soil of the tradition.[1]

What has happened to the rabbi in America? First, he has dropped out of the power structure of Jewry. Roseman comments,

It is our observation that the lay leaders of the power structure operate with only a minimal regard for the opinion of the rabbis. Their ethic is entirely secular and relates to Jewish religious norms only as an afterthought, if at all. The rabbis are consulted out of deference to their position and stature, and with the knowledge that their cooperation is necessary for the execution of many policies, but we seriously doubt whether a lay leader would relinquish his own vital interests or change well-established community policy on the advice of a rabbi. We are aware that, in many communities, rabbis have headed the local welfare fund drives and other communal projects. Such an occurrence would be impossible in our sample community, where the laity is so firmly entrenched in power.[2]

[1] Stuart E. Rosenberg, *The Search for Jewish Identity in America* (New York: Doubleday Anchor Books, 1965), pp. 258–60, 262–63, 265–66.

[2] Kenneth D. Roseman, "Power in a Midwestern Jewish Community," *American Jewish Archives*, XXI, No. 1 (April, 1969), 81–82.

Dropping the rabbi out of the decision-making circles of the Jewish community merely took account of the rabbi's profoundly different role. Formerly judge, administrator, holy man, scholar, and saint, in American Judaism the rabbi at first served as a rather secular leader of a rather secular community, spokesman for Jews to Gentiles, representative of his synagogue to the larger Jewish group, agent of Zionist propaganda, and certifier of the values of the upper-class Jews who employed him. But as time passed these roles and tasks passed into the hands of others, better equipped for them because of community position, economic power, and public acceptance. The rabbi was left to preside at circumcisions, weddings, and funerals, to "conduct" religious worship, which, in traditional synagogues, meant to announce pages and tell people when to stand up and sit down, to counsel the troubled and others marginal to the life of the community, and to teach the children, in all a slightly ridiculous figure, a medicine man made obsolete by penicillin.

But that is not the whole story. With the decline of the effectiveness of educational enterprises, the rabbi, who normally was nearly the only Jew in town who could read Hebrew and intelligently comprehend a Jewish book, stood forth for the same reason as in classical times—because of his learning. So far as access to Judaic tradition and capacity to comprehend Judaic thinking proved important, the rabbi continued to hold the key to the mind and intellect of Judaism. Second, and still more important, the rabbi could be made into a pathetic remnant of ancient glories of his office, but he remained the rabbi. The title and the role persisted in setting the rabbi apart from others, in making him a kind of holy man. In psychological terms, he continued to function as a surrogate father and God. Secularity did not, could not in the end, deprive him of his role as a religious figure, even leader. The holy man remained just that, even to the most secular people.

How have rabbis responded to the present role accorded to them in Jewry? The most interesting response comes from a rabbi acutely attuned to the power realities of the community. Hertzberg points out that in an earlier era rabbis might have wanted and enjoyed the political and cultural prestige now no longer available.

> A generation ago, the overwhelming majority of the rabbis in America were either immigrants or the children of immigrants. Even the rabbis of English speaking congregations, many of whom were chosen in part because they appeared to be completely Westernized, were thoroughly at home in Yiddish, and with the exception of one segment of the Reform rabbinate, the rabbis of all persuasions were, overwhelmingly, fervent and devoted Zionists.
>
> The great rabbinic careers of the last generation were not really made in congregations. To be sure, men like Solomon

Goldman in Chicago, Abba Hillel Silver in Cleveland, and Israel Goldstein and Stephen Wise in New York were the rabbis of imposing congregations. Their careers did not, however, unfold on the stage of what they were doing within their synagogues. Several of these men did indeed, at some point, come to high office within their specific denominational groups, but that was incidental and often as a consequence of other battles. When Silver became the president of the Central Conference of American Rabbis (Reform), in the 1930's, that was understood within the Conference itself as symbolizing the turn of its majority toward Zionism. His elevation did not occur for internal, denominational reasons. In the minds of everyone the great rabbis of that period had individual synagogues as their base, but they served as such to exercise what was essentially political leadership, in the Jewish community and on its behalf in American politics and in international Jewish affairs. Silver is again perhaps the best example. He remained a factor in Republican politics, because he could and did produce the necessary Jewish votes in Ohio, especially for his friends in the Taft family. As a Zionist leader he translated this power into political leverage against Franklin Delano Roosevelt, when the latter faltered on Zionist issues. Stephen Wise led the Reform elements in New York against Mayor Walker. He was as much the leading Democrat among the rabbis of the country as Silver was the leading Republican, and the defeat of Wise by Silver for the leadership of the American Zionist movement in 1946 represented, more than anything else, the disillusionment of the Zionists with a policy of trusting the Democrats.

The American rabbi of today is quite clearly a different phenomenon. There exist today many individual congregations as large as or larger than the congregations headed by Wise and Silver. Nonetheless, no comparably renowned rabbinic names have emerged. There are a few specialized reputations in Jewish scholarship, but it is a well known fact that the scholars among the rabbis have no real power in Jewish communal affairs. There is hardly one rabbinic figure today who commands the attention of the entire Jewish community. This is so at the very time when the majority of the Jews of America are formally affiliated with the synagogue, and when both locally and on a national scale American Jewish life has been prospering. The organized enterprise that the rabbis head, the synagogue and all its institutions, is more powerful than ever before, but the rabbis seem to be less so. Why?

Part of the answer lies in the very "success" of the synagogue. All enterprises in America today—economic, political and religious —have been undergoing the same shift from viable, small private enterprises to institutionalization. Careers which in the past were made through personal force and creativity, have now been transmuted into advancement for service to large organizations. The successful owner of a local grocery store of a generation ago is today the manager of a division for a chain of supermarkets, looking forward to the day when he will be a vice-president of the company as a whole. The very success of the religious institutions in America implies that the central bodies are now much stronger and that they have much more influence—to be blunt, they have many more favors to grant and they are much less beholden to powerful, individual rabbis. On the contrary, those individual rabbis who have the normal, human ambition to rise must now take much greater account of the wishes and the needs of their central denominational bodies.

A generation ago, the central organs of religious Jewish life were largely dependent for moral and material support on the good will of potent individuals, both lay and rabbinic. Now these bodies are so large that they are ever less beholden to any individual. They can, and indeed do, bypass even the most powerful rabbi and deal directly with his congregation and community. This means that status within the general community, and sometimes even within an individual congregation, is much more affected today by the relation of the rabbi to his denominational superiors than it was a generation ago. The result is that rabbinic careers today are evermore being made in semi-bureaucratic fashion. They tend to be safe rather than picturesque.

The people who are occupying the pews of individual congregations also differ from their parents of a generation ago. In the earlier relationships there was a distinct aura of respect for learning that suffused the encounter between the rabbi and his congregants. This involved not only Jewish learning; it also involved secular knowledge. The rabbi belonged to what was then a small minority of American Jews who had gone to college, and the shop-keepers who sat before him gloried in both his rhetoric and his English accent. On the level of secular learning, the congregants of today are as well educated as their rabbi. The congregations are studded with professional people who have spent as many years in graduate schools as did the rabbi, and some of them read much more widely than he does. In the mind of the congregation, the rabbi therefore no longer enjoys a unique estate. The congregants presume that the highest reaches of learning in the rabbi's profession, as in theirs, are not being cultivated by him, but by research students. On literary, social and political matters they delight in correcting his misquotations from Yeats, or from the lead article in the latest issue of a quality magazine. The rabbi is decreasingly a man apart. Like many of his congregants, he is in a service profession. (This point is even demonstrated by the rhetoric now in vogue for the announcement of new rabbinic appointments. In the past the rabbi was usually "called" to be the "spiritual leader"; nowadays he is generally "elected" by the board to "serve" as rabbi.)

This structure of denominational life, both within the national bodies and the individual synagogues, thus tends to depersonalize the rabbi. There is far less relationship today between the individual talents of the rabbis and the fortunes of their synagogues. A growing neighborhood, with a reasonably affluent Jewish community of child rearing age, produces, as a matter of course, a large and busy synagogue. Such synagogues succeed just as well as institutions with rabbis of little personal stature—men of drive and learning are not indispensable to their fortunes. A generation ago every major Jewish center in America had at least one rabbi whom people came to hear from all over the city, Sabbath after Sabbath. Joshua Liebman in Boston and Milton Steinberg in New York had the last such congregations, in which their particular pulpit was a sounding board which an entire community heeded. Men of equal capacity are preaching today. Within their congregations on a Sabbath one finds the same human material as in the pews of their more conventional colleagues: the small group of regulars, and the relatives of the Bar Mitzvah. But there is not a single pulpit in America today which leads opinion, precisely because the attendances are institutional rather than substantive.

What I have been describing, so far, are aspects of social change in the American Jewish community as these have been affecting the role of the individual rabbi. Such is the new context of his labors; but it is not the heart of the matter. The essence of the problem that confronts the American rabbi today, much more sharply than it was ever faced by his predecessors, is the question of faith and purpose. To what end can the rabbi really lead?

The crisis of Jewish faith is a long standing one. It is at least two centuries old. In its starkest form, it boils down to the question: If one rejects orthodoxy, why be a Jew at all? This is the Jewish version of a question that has been confronting all of religion in the age of modernity: What is the role of faith among men whose primary concerns are of this world? The dominant answer among all the faiths has been that the contemporary function of religion is to play some significant role in the remaking of society. In the nineteenth century, and in the first part of the twentieth, western Christianity addressed itself, in the name of the "social gospel," to the woes of the underprivileged. In America today the most advanced churchmen make it their prime business to be on the barricades in the battle for racial equality.

In Jewish circles the equivalent of this "social gospel" has been the continuing battle of the Jews to reorder their own situation in the world. During the last century the rabbinate has been in the forefront of the fight for Jewish equality. In America, this battle is now over.

The Jewish community itself has few tangible problems. It would be content to stop the social clock at this moment, so far as its own interests are concerned. The rabbinate, therefore, has no local Jewish social tasks left. The remaining issues concern the relationship of American Jews to other communities, especially to the Jews of Israel and to the Negroes in America. Both of these cares involve basic issues and Jewish commitments, and rabbis are inevitably in the middle of the several battles. Nonetheless, it scarcely needs demonstrating that the American rabbinate is very much less involved in Zionism today than it was two decades ago. It is equally clear, despite the presence of rabbis in places like Selma, that race relations are not today the major cause preoccupying the American rabbinate. There is nothing in the tenor of rabbinic involvement in the Civil Rights issue which resembles the urgency and singleness of purpose with which many of these same men picketed Great Britain twenty years ago, when they were still students at the seminaries. In their heart of hearts the majority of American rabbis are ambivalent, for very serious reasons, about all the immediate, tangible issues of this day.

Since the synagogue in America is, to a large degree, a "Parent-Teacher Association" of its religious school, the rabbis regard with alarm any serious drifting of Jewish educational facilities, especially those for the young, outside their orbit. There are no doubt sound reasons for this attitude. From ancient times, the synagogue has been conceived of as a place of study. The rabbi is the one professional Jew best qualified by scholarship and training to concern himself with the perpetuation of Jewish learning and traditions.

However, counter-arguments from history and tradition are possible. In the past, Jewish education has been the concern not of individual synagogues as institutions which charge membership fees, but rather of the entire community of Jews resident in one locality. A good case could be made for the proposition that it would be "good for Jews" in our day, regardless of the economic consequences to synagogue institutions, that the total Jewish community organize a network of free schools for all Jewish children. Whenever such a notion is broached, it immediately becomes clear that there is one fundamental objection: the synagogues must oppose it. Regardless of the professionally treasonable thought of a few rabbis (these men are the rabbinic equivalent of the few American doctors who dare to say a good word for socialized medicine), the rabbinate as a whole will not stake its career in this generation on creating a new structure of Jewish educational and cultural institutions which will bypass their synagogues. That such a venture may be announced under Zionist auspices does not make it more likely to succeed.

For Israeli Zionists, and for a handful of American Zionists, cultural work means propaganda for *aliyah* [emigration], i.e., that even Jews in America live in spiritual exile, and that they ought to return to their natural home. The merits of this position need not detain us here. It is enough to state that, on ideological grounds, such Zionists have an excellent case, for Zionism does indeed mean that the idea of the Jews as a lasting minority outside their homeland is an anomaly. But the overwhelming majority of the Jews in America today regard this idea as subversive. For them, their rise to middle class affluence and to cultural acceptance in the last two decades has been the culmination of their dream of "at-homeness." The hundreds of synagogues that have been built were not constructed to be temporary. Here, the rabbi performs a new function. He is no longer the tribune of an embattled Jewry, as Martin Luther King is of the Negro, demanding justice on behalf of the "we" from the "they." The rabbi of today is expected to symbolize the new Jewish role as part of a new American "we." Such a rabbi may still have a good word to say for the *aliyah* to Israel of a handful of Jews from America, as a kind of continuing Jewish peace corps, but even that he will say with some circumspection. Being human, the rabbi knows that one of his bright young people might ask *him:* if *aliyah* is so important, why don't *you* go? Here, too, Zionism becomes a threat. The rabbi can maintain some peace with his Zionist past, or with some of his rabbinic frustrations in the present, by keeping a small candle burning for the notion of *aliyah,* but this, too, cannot be a Zionist career for the American rabbinate.

Can the rabbinate survive in its present form and with its present functions?

I think not, because we are now at an historic turning. The rabbinate that Jews had known for two millennia ended in America within the last decade. This hardly noticed event is as historic a turning as the beginnings of the rabbinate in ancient Israel, when the priests of the Temple lost the leadership of Judaism to the nascent class of Pharisaic teachers.

The rabbinate arose then as a new leadership, which the Jews were willing to accept, because the rabbis were the arbiters of a system of religious values which commanded their assent. While the early Pharisees were rising to dominance during the last years of the Second Temple, the priesthood remained, and it continued to perform ritual functions, but these activities became ever more vestigial. The business of Jewish life then became the cultivation of the values commanded in the Talmud, as interpreted by the scholars within that tradition. At the dawn of Jewish modernity, in the nineteenth century, the rabbinate secularized this role for a century or so, as it led the Jewish community in the name of immediate "this world" values which an oppressed minority shared: its quest for freedom and equality.

The rabbinate today is, essentially, neither judge nor leader. It is the agent of a remaining powerful and pervasive emotion about Jewish togetherness. The purely religious function of the rabbi has been becoming ever more vestigial for many decades. Indeed, it is as far now from the center of Jewish mass consciousness as were the ritual functions of the priesthood of old. The rabbi's more contemporary role as leader of the Jews in a hostile world, or as moral guide to their political action, is constantly diminishing. He has become peripheral to the major social struggles of this age.

The rabbinate thrived for many centuries by offering Jews a vision of themselves as the servants of God. It then carried on, for a relatively short time, by holding up the dream of the Jews as servants of their own quest for freedom and, therefore, as trailblazers for all the oppressed. The Jewish community within which the rabbis are working today sees itself, for the most part, as the servant of its own survival. There are no great, individual rabbinic careers, because there are no shared Jewish purposes on the American scene grand enough to evoke them.

And I see no sign of such purposes on the horizon.[3]

Hertzberg speaks of a time not long past, in which rabbis by virtue of their rabbinical positions stood at the vanguard of the Jewish community. But he rightly stresses that the great careers did not rest upon the synagogue, but outside of it. Today, the rabbi serves primarily his congregation. In a sense he has become a more religious figure than earlier. That means, to be sure, he has less power in Jewish communal affairs. But it is likely that he now enjoys more *influence* than before, and influence in shaping the ideas and purposes of others represents significant power to achieve concrete ends. The rabbi does not stand at the head of organizations, of community bureaus. But he stands behind those who do, for Jewish leaders nearly universally belong to synagogues and rely upon religious rites at least at the time of life crises—birth, puberty, marriage, death. They are accessible to the rabbi's words.

Above all, they are under the spell of the rabbi as a holy man, in a way in which the passing generation was not. To be sure, lay people are as well educated as the rabbi in many ways. But in respect to the knowledge of Judaism, standards of literacy have so fallen that the

[3] Arthur Hertzberg, "The Changing American Rabbinate," *Midstream*, XII, No. 1 (January, 1966), 16, 17, 18, 19, 22–23, 24–25, 29.

rabbi now predominates in precisely the one area appropriate to his calling. So far as people remain Jews, they depend more than ever upon rabbis to explain to them why and what that should mean. Hertzberg properly stresses the crisis of faith. At the same time, one should underline the commitment to "being Jewish" which has survived that crisis for two hundred years—a long time indeed—and seems likely to continue to flourish. It is an inchoate, amorphous commitment. But it moves people to do things they otherwise would not do. And, as I said, it is the rabbi who retains the prestige and the learning to fill that empty commitment with purpose and meaning.

The real foundations for the rabbinical position are the convictions people retain from archaic times about holy men, set aside for God and sanctified by sacred disciplines. In archaic times the rabbi was a holy man because of his mastery of Torah. Today the rabbi remains a holy man for that very reason. Thus far we have seen the sociological side of that holiness: The rabbi continues functionally to dominate because of his knowledge of Torah. But there is a psychological side as well, perhaps of more profound meaning.

It would be a gross error to interpret the rabbi as a holy man bereft of his holiness. The following paper by Richard L. Rubenstein does not, according to the author, "describe an actual case history; it is a composite picture of various facets of the perplexities and problems, internal as well as external, which color the rabbi's life and work. These observations apply to no one rabbi, though parts reflect the inner turmoil of many rabbis, including myself. I have used this fictional portrait as a device wherein I can best communicate opinions and conclusions which I have drawn from my visits with rabbis in many communities and my studies in the area of the psychoanalytic interpretation of religion." Rubenstein, in "A Rabbi Dies," describes the role of the rabbi and the psychological realities that explain that role.

He was a good man and he was dead. We expected it. Still, it was a shock. He had had a series of heart attacks. I don't remember how many. He puzzled us. The doctors warned him that they could not be responsible if he resumed work too soon, but he insisted on returning to his desk after each attack. He broke bread at the Men's Club brunch; he reviewed the latest novels for the Sisterhood; people died and he was there; he officiated at a Bar Mitzvah every Saturday; he made the hospital rounds; no committees of the congregation felt entirely adequate without him. He should have taken six months off to recuperate. Instead, the heart attacks recurred. He couldn't rest until his body gave out.

Why did he keep going? Was he so insecure after a lifetime of rabbinic service? There were men in his congregation who could have helped him with the preaching and the pastoral work. He must have known that no man is indispensable. Today another man does what he did. Life goes on—rabbis die; congregations have a way of surviving.

Did he want to die? There are kinds of suicides. There are the big suicides like jumping out of a window or cutting one's throat. They are untidy. Society doesn't approve because the victim confesses his sense of failure too loudly. There are also little suicides, an ulcer, chronic overweight, hypertension, perhaps cancer, and the biggest little suicide of them all, the coronary. Not every coronary is a little suicide. Nevertheless, some coronaries are the body's final consent to the soul's craving for rest after a bitterly disappointing life.

He seemed to have everything to live for. His children were married. He had a large congregation, one of the largest and most affluent in the country. He had a beautiful home, the one the new rabbi now lives in. He had a respected position in his community and in the Conservative Movement.

Was he afraid they'd fire him? It wasn't very likely. One doesn't fire a rabbi for getting heart attacks. Yet, he had no sense of personal security. He kept a phone at his bedside, hardly a wise thing in a heart case. At first people were thoughtful about calling him. They inquired about his health. Within a short time his hospital room became his office. All the currents of human emotion in the congregation swept to him over the phone.

There was the subtle pressure to get back to work: "Keep away as long as you need to, Rabbi. We want you to get well, but as soon as you get back, we'll have to discuss . . ."

"We always hoped that you'd officiate at Jack's Bar Mitzvah. Of course we understand . . ."

"They're sitting *shivah* for Abe Frank. Maybe you'll send a card from your bedside . . ."

"The holidays won't seem the same without you . . ."

Perhaps it wasn't insecurity that kept pulling him back to his work. There may have been a deeper threat he couldn't tolerate, a threat more devastating to him than death, the threat of free time for self-examination and self-confrontation. Perhaps he wasn't afraid to face himself; perhaps his satisfactions were genuine. Nevertheless, he seemed to have preferred busy-ness and death to insight. He may have realized that he had worked his entire life for a kind of recognition which ultimately meant nothing to him. Nothing others said or did could change the way our rabbi felt about himself. Actually, he probably didn't feel very good about himself and, in all likelihood, his death was not entirely accidental. He may have at least consented to it. I suspect that something within him yearned for it.

He had succeeded in the rabbinate but, in his own eyes, he had failed. He revealed himself more than he realized. Everybody knew that his life was his work. There should have been more to it but there wasn't. Like Jeremiah, he was too early destined for his role. His father had been a rabbi, as had his father before him. When our rabbi died, I remembered that he had mentioned his father on the Sabbath before Passover. He spoke of the importance of *Ta'anith Bechor,* the fast of the first born, which immediately precedes Passover. Our rabbi was a first born. He told us how his father had often impressed upon him the importance of honoring this little known but awesome fast by completing the study of a Talmudic tractate on the occasion or, failing that, by actually keeping the fast. As this fifty-year-old man spoke, I could feel the power and the presence of the long-dead father who had given him both his fundamental identity and the values he lived by. Deeply, more deeply than most men, our rabbi had spent his life seeking the approval and commendation of his dead father. As he neared the end of his own life, he still sought it and was convinced that he would never be worthy of it. Thousands of years ago the first born of our people were doomed to be the sacrificial victims of their fathers and their God. By fasting, redemption money and animal substitutes Judaism has succeeded in muting the conflict between the fathers and the sons. Nevertheless, the curse of the first born had never entirely departed from the men of Israel. We shall never know what nameless fear bound him to it. The son-rabbi never failed to observe the fast. There was something awesome about the way he spoke to us of *Ta'anith Bechor.* Nevertheless, he probably never understood the archaic fears within him which furthered his resolve to keep it.

His father had been a well-known Talmudist, born and trained in Lithuania. American Jews hardly set a premium on such men. We honor the exceptional few who are needed as professors in our seminaries. We regard the rest as impractical anachronisms. Who would be foolish enough to become a Talmudist when he could become a used-car dealer or a dress manufacturer? Our rabbi knew this. He knew all too well the enormous practical disadvantages involved in his father's career. There was as little point in becoming a Talmudic scholar as there was in starving. America needed rabbis, not *luftmenschen.* Our rabbi's grasp on reality sent him into the practical rabbinate, but, like most of his fellow alumni at the Jewish Theological Seminary, *he never regarded himself as a real rabbi.* His father had been a *real rabbi* and his family had barely squeaked by. Our rabbi did far "better" for his family than his father, but he never had his father's sense of the authenticity and authority of his role. His professional prosperity only aggravated his sense of having cheated himself of his inner dignity.

His father spoke English with a pronounced Yiddish accent. His marital life had been drab. Life had been exceedingly difficult for him, but he had a sense of dignity the son was never to know. The

Jewish Theological Seminary in New York hadn't added to the son's sense of dignity or authority. His teachers were men not very different from his father, save for their PhD's and their greater exposure to German scholarship. They lived in their own hermetically sealed world, isolated from the vulgarities, but also the realities, of American Jewish life. They were an elite group and they knew it. Many of the real estate offices, bakery shops, and dry goods stores of Main Street, America, were run by former Talmudic scholars from the Yeshivoth of Slobotka and Volozhin who hadn't made it. The Seminary professors had made it in their own eyes. Some of their success had been luck, most incomparable ability. They were very special and so they regarded themselves. They did not respect rabbis. On the contrary, they had contempt for them. They mocked their ignorance of the Talmud and their prosperity. The Seminary diploma did not carry the historic formula of rabbinic ordination. It read *rav yitkareh v'haham yitkareh*, "he shall be called rabbi and he shall be called wise." When our rabbi was a student at the Seminary, a very distinguished Seminary Talmud professor mocked the Seminary ordination: "Let them be *called* rabbis. After all, what's the harm? Someone has to do the dirty work."

The famous professor constantly implied to his students that no self-respecting man would take such a job. He told them that the Rabbinical Assembly was just a trade union for hired professionals. Really able men became professors; the others were second-class men at best. The bureaucratic structure of the Seminary and the Conservative movement emphasized the elite's disdain for the congregational rabbinate. The Conservative movement was hierarchical and episcopal in structure without having any official bishops. It didn't matter. Everybody knew that the faculty members were the cardinals and bishops; the congregational rabbis were at best parish priests. There was even a Curia and a Holy Office to deal with troublesome dissenters.

All his life our rabbi wanted to demonstrate to the Seminary professors that he really wasn't second-rate. He had a dream. He'd write the book which would show his teachers how much he really knew. Someday he'd prove to his dead father and to the living men like his father on the Seminary faculty that his mother was right, that he was the beloved wonder child who could do anything he set his mind to. Someday he would amaze them.

It was only a dream. It flickered and grew dim as the years passed. He enrolled in the Seminary's doctoral program but never completed it. He thought he'd finish his dissertation during vacations. He never did. The years passed. One day he realized it was too late. He was a washout. He'd never be half the man his father was. He'd always be a mediocrity. That year his raise was bigger than ever. It should have filled him with a sense of pride. The congregation had expressed its confidence in him in the most tangible way they knew. On the surface he was pleased, but somewhere within he hated himself for his raise. It seemed unearned and undeserved. He couldn't let the world know the truth, but he knew: He was a fake-rabbi, a fraud, in his own eyes.

He never got to know himself. He was a driven man and he paid a terrible price. When he was a very small boy he thought he caught a rare glimpse of his mother's woman-need for her man. It was a terrible shock. The next day he had forgotten the glimpse. It was as though nothing had happened, but everything had changed in that instant. He'd never be as good as his father. His mother would never express her woman-need for him. He became second-rate in a moment he could never remember but which never left him. His first reaction was murderous, uncomprehending rage. He'd kill his father. The thought was hideous, so hideous that he could never acknowledge to himself that he had it. There was only one way out. If he couldn't kill his father, he'd become like him. He, too, would be a rabbi. He'd never succeed in really being like him, but, if he came close enough, he might someday possess a woman like his mother. He'd never be as good as his father and his woman would never be as good as his mother, but what could a second-rater hope for? He'd always be mediocre. His father would always be the bigger and better man. Still, the hope never left him. If he could only find his way back to mother and her woman-love, he'd never be a second-rater again. She had been dead for years, but he never gave up hope. And, he never knew what it was he hoped for. It was the book, the doctorate, the love he thought his congregation withheld from him, but behind all the proofs of worth which always evaded him, he continued to seek an assurance he never understood.

The rabbi and his wife seemed like a perfect couple. She came from a rabbinical family, as did his mother. Truth to tell, the resemblance was there. Of course, he didn't think much of those new psychological theories which saw incest in every decent feeling. Life in the congregation was difficult. The world had never expended much love on Jews. Jews couldn't easily hit back at those who treated them harshly. Like the blind man who instinctively smiles when he feels his anger rising, Jews are afraid of their anger. A two thousand year old crime poisoned their relationships with Christians. Even two thousand bishops couldn't really change things. There were times when they had to hit back at someone. The rabbi was a perfect target. He did not dare to retaliate. It could have been at a committee meeting. An objection was raised, not for the sake of the objection, but for the sake of wounding the rabbi. It could have been at a social occasion. Humor can be vicious. The occasions were legion. The rabbi quickly learned the lesson. He could as little afford to return his congregants' hostility as they could afford to retaliate against gentile aggression. He was the congregation's Jew. Subtly, often unconsciously, they treated their rabbi the way gentiles treated them.

He winched, but he had to take it. "It was a rotten life," people said. "It was no job for a Jewish boy," they laughed, but he had to take it . . . and smile.

Things might have been easier if he had been able to come home and find comfort there. She was a good wife. She provided his meals. She kept the house clean. The furniture was always in good shape. People liked her as a hostess, but something was missing. She had her own reasons for thinking she too was second-rate. Her parents wanted a boy. Every Jewish mother wants boys, not girls. Every Jewish mother is under the illusion that their daughters do not understand their mother's disappointment. In her household, boys became rabbis. All that she could do would be to marry a rabbi. That wasn't nearly good enough. As she grew up, she saw the difference between the way her parents treated her and the way they treated her brothers. Her brothers' Bar Mitzvahs made her angry. Unaccountably, she became hostile at these celebrations. Nobody could understand it, least of all herself. Her brothers went off to the Seminary to become rabbis. The family talk was about them and their accomplishments. Little was said about her. Sometimes she thought she had to atone for some nameless sin. Sometimes, she thought the nameless sin was the crime of being a woman. She never wanted to be a woman. She never learned how to enjoy a woman's feelings.

As a girl she wasn't bad looking, but her body infused her with stirrings which made her afraid. She knew that she was supposed to be a "good" Jewish girl and that she had to be careful. She knew girls who were pretty loose but she was determined to be a "good" Jewish girl. She watched herself and she kept her body in check. She never really gave in to her feelings. And, she became ever angrier, an anger she never dared to show. Their courtship wasn't very long. Their lives had been predestined for each other. The marriage was inevitable. She came from the "right" kind of family. She knew what was required of a rabbi's wife. She was the logical choice. He was already ordained. He was a friend of her older brother. He had a promising career before him. Theirs would be an excellent *partnership*.

The match had logic, but I am not sure it ever had much love. Nobody ever really knows what goes on between two people, but there are a number of things about their lives about which I have often wondered: They both had such unfulfilled faces. Did they get any real pleasure of life? Was their bed a place where they found release or were they tortured by an intimacy which was in fact a terrible wall forever separating them? His life was difficult outside. Did he find the warmth and comfort in sexual union which would have given him the confidence to face a difficult and problematic vocation or were the frustrations of his role multiplied by the more devastating frustrations of his intimate life? Could a clean house and a good salary compensate for a fundamental lack of deep sexual gratification?

People regarded him as a successful man, but his life was different from that of the other successful men in his community. There were a lot of unhappy marriages in his congregation. Several of his board members had taken mistresses, often from among their gentile employees. The rabbi unknowingly envied these men their out-of-town trips and their greater sexual freedom. Occasionally, a woman in his congregation would consult him about her inner discontents. Sometimes, these women stirred him. They wanted a man; they wanted him. His wife never seemed to value him *as a man*. She never experienced any pleasure in their intimacy. A favorite theme of his wife's conversation was "If only they knew you as I do. . . ."

The temptation to have an affair was there but nothing ever happened. He was impressed by the old rabbinic legend that Joseph was prevented from accepting the invitation of Potiphar's wife because the image of Jacob, his father, appeared before him in the moment of temptation. The image of our rabbi's father was always there. It made him feel continually mediocre. It infused him with guilt for the longings of his unfulfilled body. It made him hate himself for lusting after women he'd never touch.

He was desperately afraid someone would find him out. The rabbinic image had to be preserved at all costs, but sometimes the strain between his own image of himself and what he hoped his congregants would think of him was too great to bear. He experienced moments of anger and fury born of his inner frustrations. He could not look at his wife in the bed without a measure of disgust. Was this the reward of an observant Jewish life or was this the prison to which he had condemned himself without hope of escape? She looked so unappealing lying there. Age had not improved her looks. He never realized it but there were times when he wanted to kill her. He was a rabbi, but he was also a man with body yearnings. As he grew older and death became, not something that happened to others but something that would soon happen to him, his sense of desperation grew ever greater. He insisted on middle-aged, unattractive secretaries in his office. He could not bear to have attractive young women around him although he could never admit this to himself.

I always used to wonder why he spoke continually of the beauty of Jewish life in Eastern Europe before Hitler in his sermons. There was an incredible nostalgia in his preaching. I came to realize that *he was not urging his congregants to live his kind of life but his father's*. He called upon his congregants to return to a lost world as his way of expiating his own guilt at having left it.

Preaching was difficult. He seemed convinced that the ills of the Jewish community derived from their having forsaken his father's kind of Judaism. His basic message was always the same: "Return to the life of Torah; don't be taken in by the rootless, vulgar commercialism of the world of buying and selling; in Judaism you'll find the sense of worth, assurance, and dignity your lives no longer possess."

It was not an easy message for him to deliver because he was closer to the life he preached against than the one he urged upon his congregants. He hardly wished his life on anybody. He told his people to give up the externals, but he wanted the very externals he belittled. He was more like his congregants than he was like his father, and he despised himself for it.

There were times when all his anger and frustration were condensed into passionate sermons of moral condemnation. He berated American Jews for their shallowness and their materialism. When he became angry, he could make us squirm with intense discomfort. One day I realized that he was furious at us as he spoke, that he hated our being like him. I also saw that there was something sadistic about his condemnations. Nevertheless, I was surprised by the reaction of the congregation. *The people never appreciated him more than when he lacerated them.* They felt guilty and they wanted to be punished, provided that they did not have to take the punishment seriously. They often came to the synagogue just to be scolded. They too had fathers whom they could never appease; they too despised themselves; they hated themselves for the tawdriness of their lives.

They also hated themselves for being Jewish; they hated themselves for their money and for the way they earned it. They possessed more than their fair share of anxiety and guilt. If their fathers were no longer alive to whip their bare behinds for stealing the cookies of life, they had to set a father over them to do it for them. Our rabbi's anger at his own unfulfilled life harmonized with their need to be punished. They were tied to each other by bonds deeper than they could ever understand.

I never had much to say to him. We were both Jews, but we lived in such totally different worlds. I loved our services, largely because of the cantor and the music. I came regularly but found his preaching boring. I saw life as somewhat more complicated than simply learning how to become like his father. Still, I remember him with affection in spite of all that separated us. When my father died, he called on us. I was more consoled by his simple presence than by anything anyone else said or did. The fact that he was there was sufficient. In a way, it was just as well that we didn't have much in common. What would have been the point of our discussing Buber, whom he couldn't understand, Sartre, whom he regarded as a sick nihilist, or Freud, whom he saw as sex-obsessed?

He visited me at the local hospital during my brief illness. Hospitals are never pleasant places. Their antiseptic sights and smells are hardly conducive to good cheer. Without knowing it I had become depressed and felt abandoned—until his visit. We talked small talk. I suppose he wasn't exactly pleased that he spent so much of his time in chatter, but it was the only kind of conversation which worked in the hospital room. By his visit he told me, "You are neither abandoned nor unloved. I come to you on behalf of your friends and your community." Of course, he didn't say this explicitly, but that was what his visit meant to me. I was totally unaware of it before his visit, but I needed him and I was grateful. His dull, pedestrian sermons hardly mattered. What did matter was that he was there.

At times he had to be a magic helper. I had no doubt he had conflicts about being both priest and witch-doctor. I saw his magic work one time in a way I'll never forget. A friend of mine had a ninety-four-year old grandmother who had just lost her sixty-four-year old son. When I came to pay a condolence call, she was in a horrible condition. She was cursed with an alert mind and felt the loss of her eldest son more acutely than most younger women. She hadn't eaten for three days and kept on moaning, "Why didn't God take me first?"

The rabbi came in. She managed a brief word. He tried to say the right things, but it was obviously difficult. I didn't envy him the task. He asked her whether he could pray for her. She nodded. He read psalms which praised God for his righteousness and truth. The old woman nodded agreement. She joined him in praising the righteousness of God. The effect was unbelievable. Ritual had helped both the rabbi and the woman. Her only hope lay in accepting reality so that she might turn from the loss to finding some happiness with her other children, grandchildren and great-grandchildren. Nobody could have helped her by simply telling her, "You must accept reality." That would have been too verbal and too intellectual. His prayers and his reading of the psalms brought her to acceptance and consolation. As she followed him in affirming the righteousness of God, she reminded herself that, though the world did not conform to her wishes, all was by no means lost.

He promised her he would be mindful of her son when he recited the *Kaddish* before the congregation. His promise probably made him feel uncomfortable and slightly guilty. After all, he was not a medicine man and the *Kaddish* was a doxology, not a prayer for the dead. For the old woman, our rabbi's promise was almost like the assurance of eternal life for her son. She knew her son was dead, but she also knew that someone cared, that the inevitability of eternal forgetfulness would be delayed. Neither she nor the rabbi really knew what had transpired between them. When he left, she ate heartily for the first time since her son's death. At that moment, he seemed to us like a *wunderrebbe*. I know he added time to that womans' life. She is now ninety-six. I am sure that if I had asked him how he helped her, he could not have given an adequate answer, but he had bestowed the gift of life on a woman who otherwise would have wasted away in misery.

His officers were a rough, tough, hardened group. They were all self-made men. They had fought their way up the hard way. Nobody had given them anything. They had started out penniless. Many of them were now millionaires. To the gentile world, they were still just pushy, overly clever Jews, to be watched and never to be trusted. They made their money in jewelry and dry-goods, real estate and small banking. As they prospered, they realized that they were still regarded as second-class by the people who really counted in our city. They were ignored by the leading charity drives. They never acquired any social standing among the WASP elite. To the ruling WASPs they were just rich Jews, and that wasn't much.

They hadn't had it any easier with the old monied German-Jewish families who were the town's so-called Jewish elite. Actually, the German-Jewish elite had none of the characteristics of a real aristocracy. They were too busy trying to be imitation WASPs. Our board members were invited to take part in the fund-raising drives of our Jewish Charities Federation, the JCF, but they were seldom invited to sit on the board with the old German-Jewish families. The only time they saw the inside of the German-Jewish homes was at parlor meetings to raise money.

Our officers were never invited to join the Harmony Club, the Jewish city club, or the Westminster Country Club. It rankled them that they had to build their own country club, Whispering Pines. It was bigger, better equipped and more expensive than Westminster, but everybody knew it was second-class. Only the Reform rabbis were members of Harmony Club and Westminster. They made our rabbi an honorary member of Whispering Pines. He liked golf. He and his wife used to come out during the golf season, but once I heard him say, "I feel like a kept woman every time I come to this place."

The officers were rich, bitter, opinionated men. A whole life of work had brought them neither recognition nor contentment. *There was one place where their word was absolute law.* They ruled the synagogue with an iron determination. They finally found in the synagogue all the recognition they craved from the outside world. Here they were absolute masters. What did it matter that the Reform Congregation was more fashionable? They were more Jewish! Maybe the Germans had a real country club. They had a real *shule!*

The younger men in our congregation complained that the leadership never sought new blood. Why should they? They had worked hard to build what they had. They were used to buying things. In our synagogue their success was recognized, their money counted, and if they were rich enough, they could buy even greater prestige with their contributions to the Jewish Theological Seminary and the United Synagogue of America.

They had a peculiarly ambivalent attitude towards our rabbi. They recognized his importance and his authority, yet he was their hired hand. Many of the trustees contributed more money to the synagogue and its three million dollar building fund than our rabbi received in salary. The trustees' attitude toward our rabbi vacillated between inordinate respect for someone who took the place of their fathers and contempt for the valet. Sometimes both attitudes were intermingled. Inevitably, our rabbi missed a few sick calls. There was no greater wrath than the fury of an officer whose sickness had gone unnoticed. The rabbi's neglect triggered their deepest fears of their own irrelevance and lack of worth. They were threatened by the thought that perhaps the gentiles and the German-Jews were right in putting them down. Surely a lifetime of work was not to be repaid by such a slight!

In reality, he was always their hired hand. He depended upon their generosity and they expected their hireling to give them the prestige the world had denied them. If they had received it from the larger world, they would have been less interested in the synagogue. The world's contempt had done more than Jewish loyalty to drive them back to the synagogue whose values their lives had denied. They did not want our rabbi at their board meetings. They liked to *tell* him what to do, but they were always stopped by the fact that he was the rabbi. They could never quite make up their mind, hired hand or revered father. They never knew. When their contempt was too openly expressed they felt guilty and ashamed. They turned to reverence, but they couldn't remain respectful very long. They also knew the difference between our rabbi and a *real rabbi*. There was something almost schizophrenic in their attitude toward him. It was never consistent. He was condemned to be a man apart, a lonely man who could never forget his lonely role.

Morris Levy had been the Honorary President of the congregation for years. He had seen rabbis and presidents come and go. He had buried several. He had been the real power in the congregation for fifty years. Everybody wanted to unseat him. Nobody dared. Our rabbi quickly learned that Morris Levy was the one man in the congregation who could destroy him. Morris always maintained a surface politeness toward him, but Morris was a man of unbending will. He knew only one emotion, dominance. There had been neither love nor children in his life. Morris Levy had only one world, our congregation. He ruled it more absolutely than any eighteenth-century monarch ever ruled his kingdom.

There never was an open confrontation between Morris and the rabbi. They hated each other, but were condemned to live with each other. The rabbi never expressed an opinion on administrative policy. He could assert his authority on ritual matters, but he knew that questions involving real power were handled by Morris. He made it clear to Morris that he had no intention of fighting him. This only heightened Morris' disdain. Our rabbi was not a real rabbi in Morris' eyes. Our rabbi was not like the men Morris had met in his father's house. "What kind of a rabbi would

take orders from somebody like me?" Morris asked himself. Morris'
self-contempt made it impossible for him to respect those who
recognized his power. As a result, Morris was never satisfied. To
accept Morris' dominance was *ipso facto* proof of worthlessness.
For the rabbi not to accept it would have meant loss of his job.
By submitting to Morris, our rabbi degraded himself in his own
and Morris' eyes, but he had no choice. He knew that his father
could have handled Morris. He had watched Morris with men
like his father. They had a hold over Morris our rabbi never
possessed. His surrender to Morris preserved his livelihood, but
it deprived him of all dignity.

I shall never forget the reaction of the trustees to the news
of our rabbi's death. They were horrified and inordinately guilt-
stricken. One man told me he could not eat because he was so
sick at our rabbi's "sudden passing," as if his heart attacks had
no relation to his death. They draped our rabbi's chair in the
synagogue with black ribbon. It became a sacred place no man
could approach. Everything he used became taboo. The officers
were depressed and anxious. They spoke of him in tones of sincere
but utterly exaggerated respect. Was this their hired hand, the
man they had told to come to early morning *minyan* more often,
whose sermons they ordered shortened to twenty minutes? As I
listened to their comments and to the tributes at the various
memorial ceremonies, our rabbi seemed to become another Moses,
a saintly genius, an irreplaceable treasure. I asked myself, "Do
they really mean what they are saying? Do they believe all this
after everything that has transpired?" It didn't take me long to
concluded that *they meant every word*. As he lay dead before us,
he had become the most important person in the world to the
Yom Kippur-size congregation which gathered for his funeral. The
grief was real; the tributes sincere; the guilt unbounded.

Our congregation experienced the same sort of shock in reduced
dimensions which the nation had experienced when President
Kennedy died. Just as there had been people who had said we
had all killed President Kennedy, there were people who said we
had killed our rabbi. I dismissed the thought when somebody
confessed to me that he felt a little responsible for the rabbi's
death, but, as I thought about it later that day the idea made
sense. We were all living through the archaic ritual death of the
king. He was our primitive offering just as President Kennedy
became the nation's. The King must die and we had killed him—
long live the King. Shortly after our rabbi died, an insane young
man arose during Sabbath services and murdered Rabbi Morris
Adler of Detroit. At the time I remember wondering whether
this insane young man had acted out a temptation "normal"
people experience and then repress.

Did we wish for the death of our rabbi? I know I did if I am honest. I was glad every time he preached a mediocre sermon. It made me feel superior. I loved his failures. I was delighted with the gossip I heard about his trouble with the board. I wanted to see him levelled to the position of unexceptional anonymity in which I found myself. His sermons on the Torah angered me. I am free of that stuff. I eat as I please. I live as I please, but he still had the power to make me feel guilty for my freedom. If only I could get rid of him, I might be rid of my guilt.

I resented the fact that he always received attention that I never got. After all I was smarter than he, but that didn't make any difference. He was the rabbi. I never had the opportunity for the kind of sexual high life of a few men in the congregation. I wonder how guilty he must have made them feel. We all felt guilty and we all wanted somebody to die for our sins.

He was very observant. More than once I heard a great devotee of Chinese food in the congregation observe that while he didn't keep kosher, he couldn't respect a non-observant rabbi. There was never the slightest suspicion about our rabbi's conformity in ritual matters. He was encased in it and couldn't get out, though I doubt that he ever wanted to. Whether he did or not, *I wanted him encased in it*. I wanted to know that someone in the congregation lived according to the Law. He was doing it for me as well as for himself. I took a secret delight in the restrictions that hemmed him in. I laughed at him. It was in part my revenge for the special attention he received. He was somewhat like a king whose people revenged themselves upon him because of his preeminent position by insisting that he observe all sorts of enclosing, limiting rituals. I could understand the risks President Kennedy took with his life. He must have gotten sick at looking at Secret Service men forever disturbing his privacy. Finally, he decided that safety was too high a price to pay for their intrusive presence. Our rabbi never had to worry about Secret Service men, but he did have to worry about where he ate and what, about whether to wear a hat or not, about when to be himself, if he ever knew how, and when to retain his mask. It was our way of killing him bit by bit.

You see we wanted him dead and when he died we were frightened and guilty because he had given us what we wanted. We had fathers too and they never ceased to make us feel second-rate. If only we could get rid of our fathers.... He had taken the place of our fathers. He had become the voice of conscience they had been. He had some of the magic they had had. He was the symbol of everything that kept us in check and we hated him for it. And so, we wanted him dead.

We didn't know it. How could we? If a pollster had asked us whether we wanted to murder our rabbi we would have done violence to him. Murder our rabbi? Impossible. We loved and respected him. Look at the fine home we gave him. We just gave him the raise he asked for. We wanted him to live a long life and always be with us. We . . . we wanted him dead. We only understood it when he was dead and we couldn't eat, when we turned him into the saint he never was, when out of our unnamed and uncomprehended guilt, we pledged ourselves to projects in his memory.

We wished him dead and it got through to him. There was an unspoken covenant between us. We wanted him dead because he had been the exception in our midst. He yearned for death because he regarded his life as worthless and unjustified. Why did the priest of Diana of the woods cut the golden bough and murder his predecessor? He murdered only to be murdered. He became priest to die the death of kings. Our rabbi died the death of kings. Thousands of years had passed since the first king was murdered and eaten and it had happened again.

We said we had killed him, but that was not the whole story. We killed him but *he consented. He let us do it. He was with us all the way.* We were all accomplices. Abraham could not offer Isaac without Isaac's *"Hineni,"* "Here am I." *Our rabbi intuitively knew we wanted him dead and he gave himself.* Ironically, he never knew the real truth about himself, that he was a good man, a decent man, a man who by his deeds, the only test that really counts, had made an important difference in our lives. Because he was a good man we wanted him dead. Because he could never believe in his own goodness, he wanted to die. He was our victim. He consented.

I watched them lower his coffin into the ground. I paid my final homage as a Jew, I who had wanted him dead, I poured earth upon his grave and passed the shovel to the next in line. He had returned. He had found his peace. The rains of springtime were gently falling. Earth had claimed her child. Soon, she would give us of her fruits once again. She would give us other priests, other kings, other victims, but our rabbi was gone. He was a good man and he was dead.[4]

Our inquiry into the secular and modern brings us back to the sacred and archaic. We find ourselves back in the world of myths of holy men, people set aside for consecrated labors, who can do what ordinary people cannot. We started our study of the holy man with the consideration of a quite secular and worldly matter: What did a traditional rabbi do and how does his contemporary function differ? But we cannot understand the modern rabbi—who is so fully a response to the challenges of religious leadership in contemporary America—

[4] Richard L. Rubenstein, "A Rabbi Dies," unpublished, © 1971 by Richard L. Rubenstein, pp. 1–17.

without reverting to the psychological continuities drawing together modern and archaic men. For however much the contemporary rabbi differs from the rabbi of antiquity and medieval times, far more does he continue in roles and tasks they began. He measures himself by knowledge of Torah, and so do the people, although they may claim otherwise. He stands apart from others, set above them in ways that are not at all secular. In the midst of this world and its concerns, he represents another realm of being. People know it; they expect it; they demand it. This seems to me the most striking continuity with archaic religiosity, the most persuasive evidence that the human condition persists not much changed from archaic times. Roles change. Verbal explanations of what people do and say are not the same. The symbolic structure to which men respond seems bereft of its former supernaturalism, its earlier allusion to sanctity. Yet it would be too simple, and also quite false, to judge that the sacred has passed from men's lives. In secular terms, we cannot conclude that the experience of modernity so has changed people as to remove from their mind and imagination every sort of unworldly or other-worldly fantasy.

chapter 3

HOLY PEOPLE

THE "HOLY PEOPLE" IN ARCHAIC TIMES certainly knew who they were and confidently defined their relationship with Gentiles. Jews saw themselves as "Israel," the people to whom Torah had been revealed, now living in exile from their homeland. "Israel" was a nation within other nations. But eventually Israel would return to the holy land, with the coming of the Messiah.

Gentiles were outsiders, strangers to be respected but feared, honored but avoided except when necessary. Modern times were different. From the nineteenth century onward Western European Jews consciously entered the society of the nations among which they had lived for generations. They became German, French, and British citizens, ceased to form a separate community, and sought normal relationships both with Gentiles and with their culture.

For the immigrants to America the nineteenth-century Western European experience repeated itself. At first the Jews formed separate, Yiddish-speaking enclaves in large cities, but as time passed, they and their children moved to less uniformly Jewish neighborhoods, entered less characteristically Jewish occupations, wholeheartedly adopted the language and culture of the America they had chosen. The assimilation of Jews into American culture continued apace in the second generation, and by the third it was virtually complete. Then the question became, and now remains, What is a Jew? Who is Israel? What makes a person into a Jew? Are the Jews a religious group? Are they a "people"? A nation? The Jews thus have entered a lingering crisis of group identity, that is, they are not certain who they are or what is asked of them because of what they claim to be. And individual Jews face a severe dilemma of personal identity as well: Why should I be a Jew? What does it mean, if anything, that I am born of Jewish parents?

One important measure of modernity is the loss of the old certainties about who one is. The sense of a "crisis of identity" is a condition of being a modern man. Formerly, people suppose, men were confident of their place in the life of the community and certain of the definition of that community in the history of mankind. To be a Jew not only imposed social and economic roles, but it also conveyed a considerable supernatural story. Israel was the people of the Lord, bearer of revelation, engaged in a pilgrimage through history, en route to the promised land at the end of time. To be a Jew was to know not only who one was, but also what that meant in the economy of universal history. To identify oneself as a Jew was a privilege and a responsibility, but it was not a problem. The world posed problems to the Jew; Judaism and "being Jewish," not separated from one another, solved those problems, explained felt-history, interpreted everyday reality in terms of a grand and encompassing vision of human history and destiny. "We are Israel, children of Abraham, Isaac, and Jacob, loyal sons of the Torah of Moses at Sinai, faithfully awaiting the anointed of God." What difference did it make that Gentiles treated Jews contemptuously, despised them, maligned their religion? In the end everyone would know the truth. Before the eyes of all the living would God redeem Israel and vindicate the patience and loyal faithfulness of its disagreeable experience in history, among men.

So much for archaic times. What strikingly characterizes the imagination of the archaic Jew is the centrality of Israel, the Jewish people, in human history, the certainty that being a Jew is the most important thing about oneself, and that Jewishness, meaning Judaism, was the dominant aspect of one's consciousness.

Daniel Bell states the problem of self-knowledge, the "crisis of identity," of the modern Jew and places it into the context of modernity.

> A persistent fear worried Jews of the early Diasporas and of Hellenistic times: the fear that a child of theirs might grow up to be an *am-haaretz*—a peasant, ignorant of Torah; or, even worse, an *apikoros*—a sophisticated unbeliever who abandons Jewish faith to indulge in rationalistic speculation about the meaning of existence. In either case, the danger felt was that such an individual would not only ignore the commandments and rituals, but that

he would, in effect, have lost the sense of his past. Asked, in the classic question of identity, "Who are you?" the *am-haaretz* does not understand; and the *apikoros,* instead of giving the traditional response: "I am the son of my father" (Isaac *ben* Abraham), says: "I am I"—meaning, of course, I stand alone, I come out of myself, and, in choice and action, make myself.

A similar crisis of identity is a hallmark of our own modernity—except that not rationalism, but experience, has replaced faith. For us, sensibility and experience, rather than revealed utterances, tradition, authority, or even reason, have become the sources of understanding and of identity. One stakes out one's position and it is confirmed by others who accept the sign; it is no longer the hand of the father placed upon us—the covenant—that gives confirmation.

Not only the Jew, but all moderns, and particularly the intelligentsia, have made this decision to break with the past. Affecting first revealed religion, and later extended to all tradition and authority, the break has meant that the individual himself becomes the source of all moral judgment. But once experience is the touchstone of truth, then a "built-in" situation develops where alienation from society—which necessarily upholds the established, traditional values—is inescapable. This has meant, in the further fragmentation of society, that individuals have sought kinship with those who share both their sensibility and their experience—that is, with their own generation. The others have had a necessarily different experience. (Here we may see one reason why youth movements, a phenomenon unknown in previous times, are so characteristic a fact of modern life.)

Few of us can escape this mark. This is the way we have been bred. In us, especially the Jews, there has been a hunger for experience. The first generation fled the ghetto or the Pale—the second fled the past itself. For those of us whose parents were immigrants, there was the double barrier of language and culture to confront; and the double urgency of being not only thrust out on one's own, but having to make one's self in the course of discovering the world as home.

Yet no one wholly makes himself; nor is there such a thing as a completely cosmopolitan culture. The need to find parochial ties, to share experiences with those who are like ourselves, is part of the search for identity. There is an old truism that in some ways (biologically) we are like everyone else; in some ways (the idiosyncrasies of personality) like nobody else; and in some other ways still, like somebody else. In the parochial search for those like ourselves, the generation, the common age group, is only one tie. Neighborhood, city, country, vocation, political belief, family—these hold other ties. But prior to all—to begin with—one must come to terms with the past. One cannot wholly escape it. One may reject it, but the very mode of rejection is often conditioned by the past itself. A man is, first, the son of his father. In almost all tribal societies, the patronymic is part of one's name. And the sins of the fathers—in the psychological, if not the legal sense—are apt to be the burdens of the sons as well.

For the Jew, his relation to the past is complicated by the fact that he must come to terms not only with culture and history but with religion as well. For the religious tradition has shaped the others, providing both conscience and the continuity of fate. As an agnostic, one can, in rejecting religion, reject God; one may reject a supernatural or even a transcendental God. But as a Jew, how can one reject the God of Abraham, Isaac, and Jacob—without rejecting oneself? How, then, does a modern Jew continue to identify with the Jewish fate? And if such an identification is made and conditioned largely by experience, by a generational experience at that, what must be the consequences? The initial problem remains the religious one. . . .

A different mode of Jewish identification lies in accepting the ethical content of Judaism while rejecting the ritual. This has been the path of those who have sought to join the "human" side of faith with the potentialities of science—the path of reform. But if one is too much of a rationalist to accept Orthodoxy, one is too much of an irrationalist to accept the "merely" ethical side of religion. Orthodoxy's view of life may be too fatalistic, but that of ethical Judaism appears to some of us too shallow.

The ethical view is fundamentally syncretistic, drawing on all faiths, for to be valid, an ethical precept must be binding on every man and applicable to all men. Theologically, there is no more justification for a special Jewish ethic than for a Unitarian one, or for Ethical Culture, or for any non-ritualistic creed. The ethical dissolves the parochial, and takes away from individuals that need for the particular identification which singles them out and shapes their community in distinctive terms: terms which make possible a special sense of belonging shared by a group.

Ethical Judaism, in its often superficial rationalism, has taken some disturbing profundities of the Old Testament and transformed them into glossy moral platitudes. In ethical Judaism, a simplistic idea of human nature has led to the belief that there are few human ills which reason cannot remedy. But beyond that, the view of life represented by ethical Judaism is one of simple good and evil, unaware that a tragic component of choice is the fact that it must always involve some evil—a lesson which has been taught us by recent 20th-century history. As Emil Fackenheim once put it . . . : "In the 20th century, men—all of us—find themselves compelled to commit or condone evil for the sake of preventing an evil believed to be greater. And the tragedy is that we do not know whether the evil we condone will not in the end be greater than the evil we seek to avert—or be identified with it."

What is left, then, for one who feels himself to be a Jew, emotionally rather than rationally—who has not lost his sense of identification with the Jewish past and wants to understand the nature of that tie? A Jew, we are told by one existentialist thinker (Emil Fackenheim), is "anyone who by his descent is subject to Jewish fate"—the covenant; one who by *fate* is urged to *faith*. The ground here is still faith, though the ground is "absurd," in that the compulsions to belief are beyond one's control, shaped by descent and, therefore, by history. But this is an attempt to defend faith, not fate. Lacking faith, I myself can only "choose" fate. For me, therefore, to be a Jew is to be part of a community woven by memory—the memory whose knots are tied by the *yizkor,* by the continuity that is summed up in the holy words: *Yizkor Elohim nishmas aboh mori:*—"May God remember the name of . . ."

The *yizkor* is the tie to the dead, the link to the past, the continuity with those who have suffered and, through suffering, have made us witnesses to cruelty and given us the strength of courage over pride. However much, as moderns, we reject the utterances of authority and the injunctions of ritual, the religious link with our fellows is not the search for immortality or other consolatory formulas against the fear of extinction—but is the link of memory and its articulation. . . .

If one is a Jew through filio-piety, is such a bond strong enough? Memory has its risks. The sense of the past is often merely the present read into the past. Memory is selective, it screens out the hurts, it throws roseate hues. Remembering what happened in one's lifetime is difficult enough; uncovering the past of history is even more so.

The greatest risk of memory is sentimentality, and Jewish life has paid dearly for its sentimentality. The lachrymose recollections of the *shtetl* (which are still with us) fail to recall its narrowness of mind, its cruelty, especially to school children (to which a whole series of memoirs, such as Solomon Ben Maimon's, testify), and its invidious stratification. In the same vein of nostalgia, there are the glowing reminiscences of the Lower East Side, or Chicago's Maxwell Street—but they omit the frequent coarseness, the pushing, the many other gross features of that life. At its best, this parochial identification exists as a tie of memory through pity; at its worst, it may be the continuity of appetite—the lox, cream cheese, and bagel combinations; or through comedians' jokes.

A different form of filio-piety is in the satisfying of memory, when there is no faith, by "good works." One is a Jew, discharging one's obligations as a Jew, through membership in Jewish organizations. Here lies the second risk, of accommodation. In the *embourgeoisement* of Jewish life in America, the community has become institutionalized around fund raising, and the index of an individual's importance too often is the amount of money he donates to hospitals, defense agencies, philanthropic groups, and the like. The manifest ends are the community functions being served, but frequently the latent end is the personal prestige— *yichus.* This kind of institutional life may even lend itself to historic forms of corruption: of simony, when those who have risen high in Jewish organizations receive their rewards in appointive office in Jewish life; and of indulgences, when leadership is the simple reward of wealth. And in performance of charity as a way of Jewish life, self-satisfaction may take on the face of righteousness. The most sensitive of the Jewish agency professionals, lawyers, and businessmen have often deplored this situation, yet are trapped by the system.

But for the intellectual, the greatest risk of memory is its repression—the past is only allowed to come back in the form of self-hate, shame of one's parents, the caricaturing of Jewish traits (most notably verbal agility), the exaggerated thrust of ambition, the claims to superiority by the mere fact of being a Jew, and all the other modes of aggression that arise from the refusal to accept the tension of being in a minority, and the need to balance the insistent demands of the past with the needs of the present.

Coming to terms with this kind of repression often leads to alienation from Judaism, to the feeling of its insufficiency, even when one has some knowledge of its traditions. The alienated Jew is the Jewish orphan. He comes "out of himself," rather than out of a past. He is homeless. The present is his only reality. Lacking a past, he can have no notion of continuity, or any image of the future. For him there can be no parousia, no fulfillment. This has been the signet of Jewish fate, particularly in Central Europe, over the last forty years, and it foreshadowed the fate of a whole generation of intellectuals. As W. H. Auden once said of Kafka, "It was fit and proper that [he] should have been a Jew, for the Jews have for a long time been placed in the position in which we are all now to be, of having no home." The problem is spiritual, not territorial. Israel is no answer. The alienated Jew grew up in *galut,* and the world has been his home. Is it his fault that the world has been inhospitable—rejecting those who refuse to assert a distinctive parochial tie? Yet, in the awareness of his rejection, his life is Jewish, too: he is one of a community of exiles whose common experiences are molded by the common fate—and this becomes his parochial tie.

Finally, in this catalogue of risks, there is the risk of attrition. If, in order to give it meaning, Jewish involvement requires some encounter with tradition, so that one may be able to make choices, then succeeding generations, whose encounters are few and whose memories are hazy, must find themselves with fewer and fewer ties. They are in the most difficult position of all. It is not a question of assimilation, for that is a matter of choice, the choice of severing all ties, and one which is made consciously. Attrition is not chosen—it is a wasting away. There is a word, Jew, but no feeling. And this becomes the most tragic consequence of identification solely through memory.[1]

Despite the problems raised by Bell, people generally assume that the Jews constitute a religious group. This is the consensus of the country at large. Dennis H. Wrong points this out.

> It has often been remarked that in America anti-Semitism has never possessed even the shadow of official sanction in a country containing many ethnic and religious minorities and committed both ideologically and out of the pragmatic necessities of democratic politics to equality of opportunity. Not only has this continued to be the case, but since World War II Jews have been, as it were, themselves institutionalized as part of American society. The elevating of Judaism to equal status with Protestantism and Catholicism as the third "official" religious division in American society has largely taken place since the war. Characterizations of our civilization as "Judeo-Christian" have become standard during the same period. The increasing numbers of successful national politicians who are Jewish and the growing practice of accepting Jews along with Catholics as "ticket-balancers" to Protestant candidates for office are also noteworthy. And all this has occurred at a time when the Jews are a declining proportion of the national population and when large numbers of Jews have retained a religious affiliation that has become no more than nominal.
>
> This institutionalization of the Jews has clearly been a policy on the part of powerful elite groups in government at all levels, the political parties, the churches, professional associations and the mass communications industries. Horrified reactions to the Holocaust and awareness of and sympathy with Israel have influenced these elites, however slight . . . may have been the apparent response to such recent historical events on the part of the general public.
>
> The new public status accorded Jews seems both to ensure them of continuing visibility in American society and to reduce pressures on individual Jews to abandon their Jewish identities through what used to be called "assimilation." It is, of course, as a religious group that Jews have been recognized. Whatever the obvious advantages of this recognition, it clearly carries with it a risk from the perspective of those who contend, as did Sidney Hook some years ago, that anti-Semitism is a "Christian phenome-

---

[1] Daniel Bell, "Reflections on Jewish Identity," in Peter I. Rose, ed., *The Ghetto and Beyond: Essays on Jewish Life in America* (New York: Random House, 1969), pp. 465–66, 468–69, 470–72.

non ... endemic to every Christian culture, whose religions made the Jews the eternal villain in the Christian drama of salvation." American society has thus underwritten the survival of the ancient original objective basis of anti-Semitism, or anti-Judaism, as it should properly be called in this connection.

One may doubt whether recent efforts by both Catholics and Protestants to repudiate the doctrine that the Jews were guilty of deicide will have much effect on the laity. The trouble with the view that anti-Semitism is endemic to Christianity, however, is that the contemporary decline in anti-Semitism has occurred at a time when the importance of religious identities has clearly increased in America. American religious identities obviously do not have the same meaning they had in the past and their new significance is not of a kind that challenges the secular, post-Christian nature of our society. Still, religious conflicts between Christians and Jews over such issues as Christmas pageants in the schools are unlikely to disappear and, as the record of one such controversy in Hamden, Connecticut, indicates, they may revive among Christians many of the slumbering stereotypes of anti-Semitism.

Jews are not merely regarded by others as a religious group, but they increasingly so regard themselves. In this respect American Jews appear to have completed a full cycle, returning, with the acculturation of the East European immigrants, to the outlook of the late nineteenth century American Jewish community of largely German origin and Reform persuasion, which saw itself as a marginally differentiated religious grouping within the context of relatively complete acculturation to the larger American society. The point of view that was once called "assimilationism" is no longer advanced as such by many American Jews, perhaps because it no longer seems necessary to talk about something that is actually taking place for so many. Intermarriage and the dropping of even a nominal affiliation with Judaism are probably increasing, although without the name-changing that was so common before World War II. Persons of Jewish origin with names like, say, Goldwater, who have married non-Jews and abandoned all affiliations with Judaism or the Jewish community are likely to become more common. The very decline in anti-Semitism makes such complete but non-defensive assimilation more acceptable by removing the stigma of cowardice from it.[2]

If the Jews see themselves as a fundamentally religious community, it is not only because Gentiles tell them so, but because in the main that is how they too choose to see things. Will Herberg accounts for

[2] Dennis H. Wrong, "The Rise and Decline of Anti-Semitism in America," in Peter I. Rose, ed., *The Ghetto and Beyond: Essays on Jewish Life in America*, pp. 323–25.

the Jews' view of themselves as religious, a phenomenon of importance primarily since World War II, as a function of the third generation after immigration; but it now is obvious that the fourth generation concurs, as Will Herberg clearly shows.

The third generation played a role in American Jewry that was in many ways quite unique. Among other immigrant groups the emergence of the third generation regularly meant the approaching dissolution of the ethnic group, which the first generation had formed and the second generation had perforce been identified with. True, according to "Hansen's Law," the third generation, secure in its Americanness, was not unwilling to "remember" what the second generation had been so eager to "forget." But all that the third generation of the Italian or Polish group, for example, could, as Americans, remember was the religion of the grandfather; the immigrant language and culture and way of life were, of course, irretrievably gone. And so the emergence of the third generation meant the disappearance of the "Italianness" or the "Polishness" of the group, or rather its dissolution into the religious community. With the Jews, however, it was different. The first and second generations of Jews in America repeated the common immigrant pattern: immigrant foreignness followed by an anxious effort to overcome that foreignness and become American. But the third generation of American Jews, instead of somehow finally getting rid of their Jewishness, as the Italians were getting rid of their "Italianness" and the Poles of their "Polishness," actually began to *reassert* their Jewish identification and to *return* to their Jewishness. They too were striving to "remember" what their parents had so often striven to "forget," but the content and consequences of their "remembering" were strikingly different.

We can account for this anomaly by recalling that the Jews came to this country not merely as an immigrant group but also as a religious community; the name "Jewish" designated both without distinction. As the immigrant Jews developed their ethnic group in the United States, the same duality—and ambiguity— persisted: the Jewish community was both ethnic and religious, and was so understood by all except a few hard-bitten secularists, who tried to replace its religious character by a secular nationalism or culturalism. When the second generation rejected its Jewishness, it generally, though not universally, rejected both aspects at once. With the third generation, the foreign-immigrant basis of the ethnic group began to disappear and the ethnic group as such began to give way. Among the Jews, as among other immigrants, the advancing dissolution of the old ethnic group meant the returning identification of the third generation with the religious community of its forebears, but among the Jews alone this religious community bore the same name as the old ethnic group and was virtually coterminous with it. The young Jew for whom the Jewish immigrant-ethnic group had lost all meaning, because he was an American and not a foreigner, could still think of himself as a Jew, because to him being a Jew now meant identification with the Jewish religious community. What the Jewish third generation "returned" to was, of course, that which, as American, it could "remember" of the heritage of its forebears—in other words, their religion—but in returning to the religion it was also returning to Jewishness, in a sense in which the Italian or Polish third generation, in returning to Catholicism, was *not* returning to "Italian-ness" or "Polishness." The dual meaning of "Jewish" as covering both ethnic group and religion made the "return" movement of the third generation into a source of renewed strength and vigor for the American Jewish community.

The third generation ... felt secure in its Americanness and therefore no longer saw any reason for the attitude of rejection so characteristic of its predecessors. It therefore felt no reluctance about identifying itself as Jewish and affirming its Jewishness; on the contrary, such identification became virtually compelling since it was the only way in which the American Jew could now locate himself in the larger community. Third-generation attitudes became prevalent among all but the most "old-fashioned" elements in American Jewry. A recent survey of an eastern seaboard city of 127,000, with a Jewish community of some 8,500, found that "overwhelmingly those whom we interviewed, both young and old, wished to retain their Jewish identity. . . . This desire . . . was so strong as to constitute a firm obstacle to either assimilation or intermarriage." The survey also found—and this is of major significance for our story—that "fully 97 per cent of the adolescents [teenagers from 13 to 20, all of the third generation], when asked, 'What is a Jew?' replied in terms of religion," as against 80 per cent of the parents (mostly of the second generation). "The stressing of this fact by the teen-agers," it is cogently noted, "may well be considered indicative of the fact that they were more thoroughly acculturated than were their parents." With self-identification in religious terms almost universal among American Jews, especially the native-born, synagogue affiliation grew markedly in the decade after World War II. The expansion of the synagogue is, indeed, one of the most striking features of our time. In the smaller towns and in the suburbs, as distinct from New York and other metropolitan centers of old Jewish settlement, the synagogue came to play a particularly salient role; a very large proportion of the Jewish families belonged to it, and it was the center of community life. Even many of the older people, after years of indifference or hostility, renewed their association with it.

As the third generation began to "remember" the religion of its ancestors, to the degree at least of affirming itself Jewish "in a religious sense," it also began to lose interest in the ideologies and "causes" which had been so characteristic of Jewish youth in earlier decades. Social radicalism virtually disappeared, and the passionate, militant Zionism espoused by groups of American Jews until 1948 became diffused into a vague, though by no means insincere, friendliness to the State of Israel. The retreat from radicalism and Zionism fell in with certain larger trends in American life and was reinforced by historical developments, but the surmounting of the anxieties and insecurities of the marginal second generation undoubtedly played a major part.

Over and above, and within, the general movement for religious identification, there could be discerned, in certain sections of the third generation, a deeper religious concern, motivated by a new need for self-understanding and authenticity. Serious works dealing with Jewish faith and destiny began to find interested readers precisely among the most American segments of the Jewish community, and the response of Jewish students on the campuses and of the younger married people in their communities to the new religious thinking was markedly different from what had been customary in earlier decades.[3]

We must now ask: What are the components of the Jewish identity generally accepted among middle-class American Jews? What constitutes the self-awareness of the "holy people"?

Marshall Sklare and Joseph Greenblum, basing their findings on a questionnaire, answer this probing question.

At first glance the ideal of Jewishness predominating in Lakeville seems to be that of the practice of good citizenship and an upright life. To be a good Jew means to be an ethical individual; it also means to be kind, helpful, and interested in the welfare of neighbors, fellow Americans, and of humanity-at-large. But further examination leads to the conclusion that Lakeville's ideal of Jewishness is more than a sophisticated version of the Boy Scout who guides the frail old lady across a busy street. It is more than the practice of ethics. There is, for example, the aspect of Jewish self-acceptance: our respondents feel that in order to be a good Jew it is essential to freely and proudly acknowledge one's identity. Does this attitude, we wonder, result from the belief that Jewish existence is a great and wonderful mystery as well as a distinction and obligation which Gentiles are the poorer for not sharing? Or does it have its source in the belief that no honorable person would —either overtly or covertly—lay claim to being anything other

[3] Will Herberg, *Protestant Catholic Jew* (New York: Doubleday Anchor Books, 1960), pp. 186–88, 189–91.

than what he is? It is difficult to judge between these alternatives. All that we can say is that in other places and at other times in modern Jewish history it was not always so. . . .

According to our respondents not only is it essential that the good Jew acknowledge his identity, but it is incumbent upon him to lead a life of moral excellence. Their conception appears to be that whatever else Judaism teaches, it teaches such excellence. The true test of being a good Jew is not loyalty to the old sacramentalism but the extent to which the individual actualizes moral ideals. We do not know whether our respondents consider Jewish ethical ideals as superior to those upheld by the religions which their neighbors practice, but it is apparent that they would reject the notion that such ideals are inferior.

Do our respondents, we wonder, locate the source of their belief in moral excellence in the ethic of Judaism, or do they draw upon the ethic common to all American faiths—an ethic which transcends specific religious traditions as it merges into the aspirations characteristic of secular American culture? Our conviction is that by-and-large Lakeville Jews locate the source of their ethic in Judaism, although if pressed they might say that other faiths now share the ethic which Judaism originally proclaimed. But it must also be stated that while the ethic identified by our respondents is certainly intrinsic to Judaism it appears that the motive power for their making such an identification comes from the general culture. Nevertheless, this is less significant than the fact that they identify the source of their ethic as a Jewish one. And we are again reminded that in other places and at other times in the modern history of the Jew it was not always so.

Another significant theme is that gaining the respect of Gentiles is incumbent upon the good Jew. While it is to his self-interest to do so, more importantly he must make this effort on behalf of his fellow Jews. Gentiles will consider unacceptable behavior to be characteristic of the entire group. Thus the good Jew is under the obligation to conduct himself in an exemplary manner; each Jew represents the Jewish group and is obliged to act accordingly.

We are left with the item "Know the fundamentals of Judaism," which some 48 per cent of Lakeville respondents consider essential for being a good Jew. At first glance this would suggest the *mitzvah* of study, an exceedingly important emphasis on the Jewish sacred system. If accepted at face value this item might be considered as contradicting our earlier statements about the absence of traditionalism in Lakeville. We feel, however, that given the lack of importance accorded to other traditional patterns, agreement with this item does not necessarily mean attachment to the Jewish tradition of study as a form of worship. More likely what it suggests is that the intelligent and responsible individual has the obligation to know what he stands for; just as his identification as a citizen makes it obligatory to acquaint himself with American history and current affairs so identification as a Jew makes it obligatory to acquaint himself with the fundamentals of Judaism. In regard to the reflection of this attitude in the community it is apparent that while Jewish educational programs for adults in Lakeville are not so well attended as their sponsors desire, they are an accepted feature in all of the congregations. While the suprasocial impetus for attendance at such programs must not be denigrated, it appears that the image which the Lakeville Jew has of himself as an intelligent and responsible person is operating in respect to Jewish identity. Adult education flourishes in Lakeville; adult Jewish education is on the increase. Over all, the significant fact is that some apply the concept of intelligence and responsibility to their Jewish as well as to their general identity.

In summary, the essential qualifications for being a good Jew according to Lakeville residents are self-acceptance, moral excellence, good citizenship, and knowledge of Judaism. The acts which the good Jew is obliged to perform include advancing the general welfare, promoting social reform, and increasing intergroup amity.

Turning to the "desirable" category of the questionnaire we find that the following items rank highest:

Be well versed in Jewish history and culture	73%
Marry within the Jewish faith	51%
Contribute to Jewish philanthropics	49%
Belong to Jewish organizations	49%
Know the fundamentals of Judaism	48%
Support Israel	47%
Attend weekly services	46%
Attend services on High Holidays	46%
Belong to a synagogue or temple	44%

In contrast to the essential category of the questionaire this list is more traditional: It includes items which relate to well-established religious, nationalistic, and cultural models. Thus, such items as attendance at services, support of Israel, and knowledge of Jewish history and culture are listed. A *mitzvah* such as contributing to Jewish philanthropies also occurs. In fact many of the items on the list constitute activities and attitudes ordinarily thought of as characteristic of "survivalist" Jews, such as belonging to a synagogue, joining a Jewish organization, and marrying within the Jewish group.

How should our findings on the image of the good Jew be evaluated? Some would say that they indicate the hypocrisy of the Lakeville Jew. They would focus on such items as "Work for equality for Negroes" and point out that whereas a total of 83 per cent feel such work to be essential or desirable very few lend active support to organizations whose purpose is the advancement of civil rights. Furthermore, there has been no attempt to assist Negroes in purchasing homes in the community. Hypocrisy is not, however, the significant perspective for evaluating the gap between the image which our respondents have of the good Jew and the patterns which they follow in daily life. To stress hypocrisy is to be diverted from the most crucial aspect of these responses: the desire to retain Jewish identity and the simultaneous difficulty which the Lakeville Jew experiences in affirming actions which would help guarantee—or make more meaningful—that survival. Furthermore, it becomes clear that the actions and *mitzvot* which the Lakeville Jew affirms as most essential to being considered a good Jew are actions and *mitzvot* between man and man and that *mitzvot* between man and God assume a distinctly secondary place. Finally, the actions and *mitzvot* which the Lakeville Jew esteems most highly are found in the general culture. In sum, while the Lakeville Jew may be following certain Jewish sources when he formulates his ideals, the lack of distinctiveness inherent in his model of the good Jew is capable of eroding away group boundaries.

At the present moment the Lakeville Jew remains considerably more Jewish in action than in thought. Philanthropy is a good example of this dichotomy. Some 39 per cent consider that contributing to Jewish philanthropies is essential while 67 per cent believe that supporting all humanitarian causes is essential. To be sure almost all Lakeville Jews contribute to both Jewish and non-Jewish philanthropies, but the fact of the matter is that only 19 per cent give the bulk of their money to non-Jewish charities. While Jewish campaigns are better organized and set higher sights for givers, the philanthropic behavior of Lakeville Jews is not a result of greater efficiency of the Jewish fund-raising machinery. Rather it results from the Jews' feeling of identity. Leaving aside the fact that fund-raising techniques in the general community are becoming more sophisticated, the question which occurs is how long the present gap between action and thought in the area of philanthropic giving will survive. Will not a sectarianism which is unsupported ideologically wither away when social conditions change? Will future generations be prepared to live with the dichotomy by which the Lakeville Jew abides: a universal humanitarianism as the prime value in combination with the practice of giving priority to Jewish causes? Will not future generations attempt to reassess Jewish anguish against the anguish of others, the importance of supporting Jewish institutions against the significance of other institutions? May they not conclude that their humanitarian aspirations dictate that they place the accent on the general rather than the Jewish?

In spite of the best of intentions, it is our conviction that only a minority of Lakeville parents have been able to provide their children with substantial materials for developing such a pattern. Of course each generation must achieve identity anew. Nevertheless each new generation is in part the product of its inheritance. The meager Jewishness to which the Lakeville youngster falls heir is perhaps the true *bête noire* of Jewish life in Lakeville. Lakeville makes available the abundant life; ... in many respects it is a model community which fulfills the American dream. But, at the same time it does not provide very rich Jewish experiences for the majority of those who are socialized in its fine homes, winding streets, excellent schools, pleasant beaches, tennis courts, and—let it be said—in its religious schools. Thus many of those who are the product of the Lakeville environment will be faced with the obverse of that which confronted their grandfathers, great-grandfathers, or even more remote ancestors when they arrived on American shores. While the resources of such ancestors—in terms of money, general education, and knowledge of the American way of life—were paltry, their Jewish resources—if not always considerable—were at least sufficient unto the day. Over the generations the families of present-day Lakeville Jews have increased their financial resources, their general level of education, and their mastery of the environment many times over. While some have multiplied their Jewish resources, many have dissipated them to a lesser or greater degree. It is indisputable that the majority of Lakeville Jews would like to conserve their Jewish resources. But unless an aggressive policy of growth is pursued the Jewish resources of a previous generation inevitably decline. The press of the general environment is so compelling that instead of being conserved the inheritance from earlier generations inevitably diminishes. In sum, the long-range viability of the pattern of Jewish adjustment characteristic of Lakeville is in question.[4]

We notice, first of all, that modern American Jews stress those virtues they suppose Gentiles will readily appreciate: good citizenship, the upright life. The definition of "being Jewish" begins with ethics—the least peculiar, most unparticular, side of life. No one can maintain that ethical behavior may be defined by one sub-group in society in terms that do not apply to all others. If it is ethical for a Jew to guide the frail old lady across a busy street, it is also ethical for a Boy Scout to do so. And so being Jewish and being a Boy Scout functionally are pretty much the same thing.

4 Marshall Sklare, and Joseph Greenblum, *Jewish Identity on the Suburban Frontier: A Study of Group Survival in the Open Society* (New York: Basic Books, Inc., 1967); THE LAKEVILLE STUDIES: A RESEARCH PROJECT OF THE AMERICAN JEWISH COMMITTEE, pp. 324–27, 329–30, 331.

This is on the face of it meretricious, for no one, least of all the Jew, is prepared to say that the difference between Jew and Gentile is of such slight consequence. The substance of "Jewish identity" seems to contradict the form. The commonplace traits assigned to that identity do not explain the profound sense of difference, of separateness, characteristic of the Jews' collective life. Nor are we helped by asseverations of pride, of gaining respect of Gentiles. That tells us that the Jews are concerned for the opinion of the outside world in a way in which their forebears were not.

This leads us to still another side of the identity of the "holy people," which is peculiarly modern, but not particularly American: the rejection of being Jewish by people who are, and plan to remain, Jews. It takes the form of self-hatred, the internalization of the dislike of the unlike expressed by the majority in respect to various minorities. American Jews adopt toward themselves the attitudes of anti-Semitism, or Jew-hatred. Jew-hatred came to America with the first Jews, when Peter Stuyvesant wanted to refuse Jews the right to settle in New York, then to build a a synagogue. Its impact upon Jews cannot be separated from their view of themselves as Jews. In general it produces a dislike of those things in oneself and one's personality that are supposed to mark one as a Jew. Milton Steinberg shows this in *A Partisan Guide to the Jewish Problem.*

> If anti-Semitism is the most spectacular Jewish problem and, in a practical sense, the most urgent, the issue of Jewish morale can fairly be said to be in its own quiet fashion spiritually the most desperate. For, so long as he keeps his self-respect, an individual can endure anything no matter how grievous. But let him lose that and he will be incapable of joy, creativity, perhaps even of life itself. Wherefore, Goethe observed brilliantly, the greatest evil that can befall a man is "that he should come to think ill of himself."
>
> To this disease of the psyche, some American Jews have fallen victim. How many, no one knows; but there are at least thousands who "think ill of themselves," who suffer from shame, who are plagued by a sense of inferiority—all because they are Jews. And occasionally one meets a Jew in whom the malady is virulent, a Jew who literally hates Judaism, other Jews and himself.
>
> It is now clear why Jews should have so little immunity against this ailment. For they embody to an extraordinary degree its two preconditions. They are, in the first place, not only a minority, but a universal minority. Theirs is a dissenting religion, a distinct cultural heritage. What is more, they are constantly exposed to public criticism. Sometimes, as in recent years, this beats at them

like a sledge hammer. At other periods, it is quiescent. Quiescent but never absent. Exclusions, ostracisms, affronts are always part of their existence.

The relatively peaceful prejudice that is the normal lot of Jews is infinitely to be preferred to the wild anti-Semitism of the Hitlerian era. And yet, psychically at least, the former can be more destructive than the latter, just as the prick of a pin, under certain circumstances, can be more dangerous than its stab. For he who is stabbed will be too conscious of pain to abide it. He will attempt to pull away from, or to resist his antagonist. And if he is so bound that he can do neither, he will grit his teeth and endure, but in any case will not view his condition as normal and hence tolerable. But he who is only scratched, who is at most irritated, may grow accustomed to his discomfort and come to disregard it. In which case and before he is aware of it, the point of friction may have become an ugly, festering wound. . . .

Again, the Jew senses that just because he is a Jew, he is subject to special insecurities. Like all human beings, he must submit to inevitabilities and inexorabilities. Death and taxation are as certain for him as for anyone else. But as a Jew, he is exposed to an additional set of risks and perils. For at no time can he be overly confident as to the stability of his position. The majority group may at any hour undergo a change of heart concerning him. Given extraordinary stresses, it may cease to be fair and lawabiding. Inevitably he worries, as anyone must whose position is dependent on others. Insecurity is therefore a constant in his psychology. Under normal circumstances it diminishes almost to the vanishing point. Fears of any nature after a while begin to appear foolish when the dreaded event has failed to materialize. So, people who live on a volcano that has not erupted for some time attain eventually a fair measure of equanimity. They never lose their apprehensions altogether.

In addition, every Jew at some time or other has reason to conclude that he has been penalized for his Jewishness. If he is seeking employment, if he is a student applying for admission to a medical school, if he is an instructor who wishes to be a professor, or a parent who desires to enroll his daughter in a finishing school, or a suburbanite who would like to be a member of the local golf club—he knows that his identity multiplies the hazards and obstacles in his way. Were he no Jew, he quite naturally tells himself, he would have his desire.

Sometimes these people are quite right in their assumptions. It is their Jewishness that keeps them from achieving their purposes. On the other hand, their identity is as often altogether irrelevant. If they fail it is because of themselves, not their group. Unfortunately Jews, like other human beings, are so constituted as to be reluctant to pass adverse judgment on themselves. Hence, whether with justice or not they will hold their Jewishness at fault for whatever goes wrong with their lives.

In the light of this logic—and it is logic of a sort—Jewishness comes to be regarded as a misfortune, an unchosen but inescapable handicap, like a physical deformity. It is a mean trick played by an unkind fate. Having conceived a resentment, the Jew is very likely to direct it against other Jews. For by a continuation of the same reasoning they are by their very existence responsible for his difficulties. What is most wrong with Jews, it begins to appear, is that there is a number of them. If he were the one Jew in the world he would certainly meet no anti-Semitism. If, failing that ideal condition, the body of Jews were small enough it would never provoke unfriendly attention. There are simply too many Jews. Besides the world offers only a limited amount of social advantage to all Jewry—a sort of ration of jobs, acceptances and opportunities. From his viewpoint each additional Jew means that he has less, that at a table on which there is already not enough, another boarder has seated himself. So our specimen Jew comes to rebel not only against what he is, but against his fellows as well.

The whole story however is still not told. Two other factors, one positive and one negative, contribute powerfully toward the disintegration of self-esteem within Jews. Anti-Semitic propaganda is addressed to Gentiles, not Jews. But Jews listen, and may also be convinced by what they hear. They are persuaded that they deserve their bad repute. Does this seem incredible? Then reflect on the Jew's position. In books and newspapers, in lectures, in conversations he overhears, it is dinned into his head that he and his kind are pretty bad specimens of humanity. He is told that he is obnoxious socially, unclean physically, degraded morally. Sooner or later he may begin to reason with himself that there may be something to all this ado, that where there is smoke there must be fire.

But once again, should he reach the pass of believing that the anti-Semite has a case, he will refuse to concede that it applies to him. Whatever truth may be in it, he assures himself, must refer to other Jews. Whereupon he gets very busy scrutinizing Jews outside his circle, hoping to detect in them the vices catalogued by the anti-Semite. And, as would be the case with any group of human beings, he manages to find some Jews who are the kind he is looking for.

Now his condition is sad indeed. He has come to believe the worst of all Jews except himself and his coterie. Yet the world somehow refuses to see the distinction among Jews that is so clear to him. If he is a restrained person he will forever entertain, though never voice, the hope that Gentiles will in the end per-

ceive that he is "different." If he is less meticulous, he will be
crass enough to proclaim his exceptional nature. In any event,
he will hold himself aloof from other Jews. So by a strange turn,
anti-Semitism victimizes the Jew in a fashion anti-Semites never
conceived. It converts him to its cause.

All this would have been without effect on Jews were it not
that something has disappeared from their make-up. The medieval
Jew was subjected to a full-blooded anti-Semitism that compares
impressively with contemporary Jew-baiting. His exclusion was
absolute, his security, even of life, virtually nonexistent. Yet, whatever anti-Semitism might do to his person and possessions, it
scarcely touched him psychically. Certainly he was never seduced
by it into despising himself or his group. Against that he was
protected by his tradition. His religion invested his existence as
a Jew with intimations of eternity. Knowing the culture of his
people, identified with it, he felt that it enriched and stimulated
him. The prophets, saints, and sages of the Jewish past were his
companions. No matter what the anti-Semite might say or do, he
knew that Judaism and Jewishness were honorable and meaningful
realities. That knowledge armored his sense of worth.

For many modern Jews these preservative forces are no longer
operative. Having abandoned their religious tradition, ignorant
of the Jewish past, unedified by its present, uninspired by any
aspirations for its future, they have nothing on which to sustain
self-esteem. Jewishness to them is simply a disability. They have
lost the secret of that spiritual prophylactic which enabled their
fathers to preserve their psychic wholesomeness.

But the gravest consequence of psychic malaise among Jews,
even in this, its mildest form, is to be found in their group life.
For quite naturally, Jews who are uneasy over their Jewishness
will be reluctant to associate themselves with anything Jewish. They
will stand aloof from the Jewish community or will strive sedu-
lously to keep it as inactive as possible. They will resist the Jewish
religion and Jewish culture.

When they are exposed to instruction in Judaism, even indeed
when they themselves seek such instruction, their mind-set may
prevent the educational process from "taking." They may block
out or minimize what they learn; they may be incapable of learning at all. As thousands of children have difficulty with arithmetic
because they dislike the teachers who present the subject to them
or the schools in which it is taught, Jews forever keep repelling
Jewish knowledge no matter how it is drummed into them because they are not at peace with the core fact of Jewishness. This
circumstance, as rabbis and Jewish educators will testify, constitutes one of the largest single obstacles against imparting to Jews
a familiarity with their heritage and the will to live by it.

Everything touched by Judaism suffers in consequence. The insecure Jew may turn antireligious simply because religion comes to him through the Synagogue which is perforce a Jewish institution. Or he may manifest sympathy with every religious communion except the Jewish. Even in the Synagogue itself the process of self-repudiation leaves a trail of destruction. It impels those under its sway to seek to fashion Jewish faith and worship not after its own genius but in conformity with prevailing non-Jewish patterns. Conversely, it induces antagonism toward all distinctively Jewish forms. Many a Jew has difficulty in making peace with the most beautiful and meaningful of ancestral Jewish ceremonials simply because these depart from majority practice and in consequence are unmistakable tokens of Judaism.

Where in Jewish life can the unhappy influences of the sick soul not be discerned? Jewish education, for the child and the adult alike, is its victim. The Jew maladjusted to his Jewishness is not only, as we have already observed, himself loath to learn, he will seek to prevent instruction for others or to limit it to the barest minimum. He will frown on Jewish art, music and literature, either rejecting them out of hand or at the best suppressing whatever spontaneity and exuberance they may exhibit. Himself uncomfortable over his Jewishness, he wants beyond all else that it shall be inconspicuous.[5]

Steinberg wrote more than two decades ago, when the trauma of the Hitler period, with its American counterpart, widespread Jew-baiting, was still fresh. At that time Jews were carefully excluded from the better colleges and from whole fields of economic life; anti-Semitic stereotypes were taken for granted in literature and politics. Today much has changed. But it is a measure of how much remains the same that the effects of self-hatred continue to shape the self-assessment and the collective program of American Jews. Howard Singer writes of contemporary Jews who differ little, if at all, from Steinberg's Jews of the middle generation.

American Jewry has come to think of itself as comfortable, as solidly middle class, which, at the moment, is a fair description. But things were not ever thus. American Jewry's present economic and social status is something it has achieved quite recently.

Jews—like other immigrant groups—had a difficult time adjusting to the United States. America did not really welcome the tired, the poor, "the huddled masses yearning to be free," except in ideology and the history books. In reality labor saw those huddled foreigners in the steerage of immigrant ships as a threat to employ-

[5] Milton Steinberg, *A Partisan Guide to the Jewish Problem* (Indianapolis: The Bobbs-Merrill Co., Inc., Charter Books, 1963), pp. 115, 116–17, 117–20, 122–23.

ment, and the upper classes saw them as an undigestible mass that threatened the dominant culture.

Until the beginning of the Second World War it was enormously difficult for a Jewish student to enter a decent college, a medical school, or a law school. It was almost useless for a Jewish student to study engineering; his chances of getting a job in his field were almost nil. Jews found it impossible to find jobs with the public utilities, for instance, or with banks. During the depression Jewish girls learned to wear a crucifix when they sought jobs; without camouflage they would be turned away.

The Second World War changed things. Suddenly the country found that it needed more doctors and engineers and welders, even *Jewish* doctors and engineers and welders. And when the war was over and the economy continued to expand, there seemed to be room for everybody, even Jews, even—here and there in a modest way— even Negroes. But long before that the Jew had learned to walk softly in the country in which he was, theoretically, a first-class citizen. He had learned the right tones in which to ask for *rachmonis* [compassion] and the appropriate posture when asking. And, most important, his sense of identity had begun to fade.

Jewishness is a complex thing, full of all sorts of drives and values and loyalties, the immigrant's son reduced it to something less troublesome, to a purely religious definition, a kind of Jewish Methodism with emphasis on ethics. The immigrant's son saw liberalism as America's secular, nonsectarian religion; he hoped that espousing it would make him part of America even more effectively than showing affection for baseball. The Jewish intellectual found a way of rationalizing his abandonment of Jewish loyalties by seeing it, not as desertion, but as moral growth. By professing a vague humanism or universalism, he could justify, at least to himself, casting off the particular. This has not changed much in thirty years. In the summer of 1968, George Steiner, who teaches at Cambridge University, attacked "the barbarism of blind loyalties" and urged all men to "free themselves from the myths of nationalism and proclaim that whereas trees do indeed have roots, human beings have legs with which to move freely among each other." During the same panel discussion, an Israeli writer, Matti Meged, remarked that indeed human beings do have legs, and that the Jewish people had most often used them for running away.

The dirty little secret about middle-aged American Jews, especially those on the highest economic levels, is that many dream of being reincarnated as Episcopalians. Some are not content with dreams; the Jewish chief of a TV network may actually convert; the wealthy families mentioned in Stephen Birmingham's *Our Crowd* intermarry and have few Jewish descendants. But for most Jews so afflicted actual conversion represents too great a wrench. Many find consolation by fleeing from that which is recognizably Jewish toward such neutral interests as Ethical Culture and Zen Buddhism. Their personality patterns are precisely the same as those designated by the epithet "Uncle Tom." Jews have not as yet developed a striking, characterizing name for them, and so, since I need one for this little effort at description I will invent one: Cousin Merwyn.

Why Merwyn? Because the chances are that Merwyn's Hebrew name was Mosheh, Moses, which makes the contrast perfect. Moses, brought up as an Egyptian prince, voluntarily cast his lot with the Jewish people. But that name was considered "too Jewish" by ambitious immigrant mothers, and so they began naming their children Moe, or Morris. The Morrises evolved into Marvins, Miltons, and Myrons, and eventually into that pinnacle of gentility, Merwyn. If we were to measure Jewish attitudes ranging from self-respect through bare self-acceptance to self-hatred, it would be appropriate to put Moses at one end of the scale and Merwyn at the other.

It is easy to recognize Cousin Merwyn. He is the fellow who dismisses an anti-Semitic joke as good-humored but thinks it bad taste for a Jew to tell a funny story about a minister or a priest. He averts his eyes in embarrassment when he sees a Jew carrying a *lulav* on Succoth, but he is touched and respectful when he sees Christians carrying a similar object on Palm Sunday. Jews at a Bar Mitzvah strike him as loud and vulgar, but he thinks Italians having a good time at a wedding are happily picturesque. Every Jew knows at least one Cousin Merwyn. I know dozens. . . .

Cousin Merwyn, I've discovered, comes in two models: Merwyn Outside and Merwyn Inside.

Merwyn Outside will have nothing to do with anything Jewish. This gives him no problems whatever. In the United States there are dozens of substitute faiths and movements to suit every taste, from staid Unitarianism to the radical lunatic fringe. Merwyn Outside is usually most comfortable with a thoroughly secular, humanist liberalism. As a political theory, liberalism is aloof and pragmatic, but Merwyn Outside will often invest it with the fervor his Orthodox grandfather displayed when dancing in the synagogue at the Rejoicing of the Law. Unlike a liberal of Presbyterian background, Merwyn Outside has to put all his emotional energy into his liberalism; he has nowhere else to expend it. It will have to serve as his kinship and culture group, his ethnic and religious orientation, his hope of heaven and his social milieu. That's quite a lot to ask, even of Americans for Democratic Action.

Merwyn Outside yearns to transcend his parochial origins, and goes to great lengths to succeed. He may even be pro-Arab to prove his "objectivity." But in truth, he never considers such problems on their merits. The word "Jew" touches a live nerve, triggers a reflex, and flips him onto the anti-Jewish side of any issue.

Merwyn Inside suffers from the same malady, but in another

form. He, too, will flee his Jewishness, but his flight is disguised. His technique is to take the Jews with him, to make Jewish life less recognizably Jewish. He will join a synagogue, but suggest innovations in the religious service that make it untraditional in spirit. When they are made he will not attend anyway. He will send his child to Sunday School, and perhaps join the religious school board, but he will oppose raising the educational standards on the grounds that the children are overburdened with Public School work. He will convey the insignificance of Sunday School to the child by pulling him out of classes for Little League games. With a sparkling conscience, and always in the name of "progress" or good fellowship, he will vulgarize and corrode the institutions of Jewish life.

Merwyn Outside is merely a dead loss to the Jewish group, but Merwyn Inside is a galloping disaster. For Merwyn Inside is often wealthy, energetic, and willing to work. These qualities soon bring him into positions of influence and authority. And if American Jewish organizations have lost touch with Jewish needs, it is because Merwyn Inside dominates those organizations.

B'nai B'rith, one must remember, was established in 1843; the American Jewish Committee in 1906; the American Jewish Congress in 1917 and reconstituted in 1922. Organizations need rich men on their boards of directors, and so the leadership they attracted came from the half-assimilated, upper periphery of Jewish life. Such men resented being kept out of wealthy country clubs and exclusive hotels, and they set their organizations to the task of solving such problems. They were preoccupied with "winning friends" among the gentile community at any cost. That set the style for American Jewish organizations, and ever since ordinary American Jews have paid a high price in self-respect.[6]

The "holy people" evidently has disintegrated. First, Jews are no longer certain just what makes them into a people. Second, they see themselves as anything but holy, they interpret in a negative way the things that make them Jewish and different from others, and above all, they introduce into their assessment of themselves the opinions of the Gentiles. So the advent of modernity seems to have changed everything. A group once sure of itself and convinced of its value under the aspect of eternity now is unsure of who it is and persuaded that the hostile judgments of outsiders must be true. The "children of Abraham, Isaac, and Jacob" have lost touch with the fathers. The people of the Lord seems to have forgotten why it has come into being. Everyday reality contains for ordinary Jews no hint of a great conception of human history. It has become a long succession of meaningless

6 Howard Singer, *Bring Forth the Mighty Men* (New York: Funk and Wagnalls, Inc., 1969) pp. 227–28, 229–30, 231–32.

but uncongenial encounters. Sinai is a mountain. Tourists make the trip to climb it. The "Torah of Moses" is a scroll removed from its holy ark on the Sabbath, normally in the absence of the "loyal sons," who rarely see it, less often hear it, and cannot understand its language. The Messiah at the end of time is too far away to be discerned; anyhow, no one is looking in that direction.

It is easy enough to draw invidious contrasts between the virtues of the archaic world and the shortcomings of modernity. But since the old certainties and securities are mostly gone, one might observe that not only necessity, but choice moved Jews away from them. When Jews in Eastern Europe began to feel the birth pangs of modernity, all the more so when the emigrants came to America and plunged into the modern condition, they scarcely looked backward. Whatever virtues they knew in the old way of being did not restrain them. Something in the traditional life seemed to them to have failed, for in their thirst for whatever was new and contemporary they demonstrated that the old had not fulfilled their aspirations.

It did not have to be so, and for some it was not. Both the emigrants of the 1890's and those who came after World War II included considerable numbers of Jews who remained loyal to the tradition in a wholly traditional way. The appeal of modernity was lost on them. Still others entered the modern situation and quickly turned their backs on it. The return to religion in the decades after World War II saw considerable strengthening of orthodox commitment and conviction in American Judaism, and renascent orthodoxy did not take the modern form of surrogate religiosity, large synagogues, and impersonal professionalism, but the entirely traditional forms of personal commitment and maximum individual participation. Whether traditional Orthodox Judaism in America is traditional and orthodox in the same ways as is Eastern European Judaism hardly matters. The fact is that the classical Judaic perspective remains a completely acceptable choice for substantial numbers of American Jews. Those Jews who fully live the traditional life and adhere to the traditional way of faith seem to me to have made a negative judgment on modernity and its values. It becomes all the more striking that larger numbers—the vast majority of American Jewry—came to an affirmative opinion.

But in affirming the modern and accepting its dilemmas, American Jews continued in important modes to interpret themselves in the archaic ways. Most important, they continued to see themselves as Jews, to regard that fact as central to their very being, and to persist in that choice. As Glazer points out (page 9), that fact cannot be taken for granted. The Jews are not simply an ethnic group characterized by primarily external, wholly unarticulated and unself-conscious qualities. They are Jewish not merely because they happen to have inherited quaint customs, unimportant remnants of an old heritage rapidly falling away. On the contrary they hold very strong convictions about how they will continue to be Jews. Most of them hope their children will marry within the Jewish community. Most of them join synagogues and do so because they want their children to grow up as Jews. Above all, most of them regard the fact that they are Jewish as bearing great significance.

They see everyday life in terms different from their Gentile neighbors, beginning with the fact that to them, if not to their neighbors, their being Jewish seems an immensely important fact of life. The words they use to explain that fact, the symbols by which they express it, are quite different from those of archaic or classical Judaism. They speak of Jewishness, not Torah. They are obsessed with a crisis of identity, rather than with the tasks and responsibilities of "Israel." They are deeply concerned by the opinion of Gentiles.

In all, they are eager to be Jewish—but not too much so, not so much that they cannot also take their place within the undifferentiated humanity of which they fantasize. They confront a crisis not merely of identity but of commitment, for they do not choose to resolve the dilemma of separateness within an open society. In preferring separateness, they seem entirely within the archaic realm; in dreaming of an open society, they evidently aspire to a true accomplishment of the early promise of modernity. But if that truly open society should come to realization, one wonders whether the Jews would want wholly to enter it. For, standing at the threshhold of more than two hundred years of assimilation into modern culture, of facing a lingering crisis of identity, who would have predicted what has happened? The Jew continues to take with utmost seriousness the fact of his being Jewish, indeed to speak, precisely as did those in the classical tradition, of Israel.

And this brings us squarely before the question of the State of Israel and its place in the mind of American Judaism.

HOLY LAND

ARCHAIC RELIGIONS USUALLY FOCUS upon a holy place, where God and man come together, the focus for the sacred upon earth. In classical Judaism, Palestine ("the Land of Israel") was not merely the place where Jews lived, but the holy land. It could never legitimately be governed by pagans—thus, the continuing efforts of Jews to drive pagan rulers out of the land. There the Temple was built, the nexus of the God-man relationship in olden times. The mountains of the land were the highest in the earth. The land was the center of the world, of the universe. Jerusalem was most beautiful, most holy.

No element of the classical myth at the turn of the twentieth century could have seemed more remote from the likely preferences of nascent American Judaism. When the emigrants left Russia, they could have gone southward, to Palestine, and a few of them did. But most went west, and of these, the largest number came to the United States. Since even then Zionism was an important option in Eastern European Judaism, one can hardly regard the emigrants as Zionists. A few who were stayed in America only a while, then left for Palestine. The vast majority of emigrants came and settled down.

Now, eighty or ninety years later, the vast majority of third- and fourth-generation American Jews support the State of Israel, and whether they are called Zionists hardly matters. The sole commitment shared by nearly all, uniquely capable of producing common action, is that the State of Israel must live. Zionism accounts for the predominance of the welfare funds. To American Jews, "never again"—referring to the slaughter of nearly six million European Jews—means that the State of Israel must not be permitted to perish. But there is a second, less often articulated fact about American Jewry. Alongside the nearly universal concern for the State of Israel is—by definition—the quite unanimous Jewish commitment to America, to remain Americans. Emigration to the State of Israel since 1948 has been negligible. Indeed, until the present time more Israelis have settled in America than American Jews in Israel.

When did American Jews become Zionists? Does the change testify to a new development in Judaism, or to a new experience in America? Oscar and Mary Handlin supply a succinct but definitive answer.

> The thought that the Jews of the world might, by taking political action immediately, come back to Palestine and establish a national home there had at first not been well received in America. It ran counter to the whole Reform movement, which rejected the idea of a Jewish state. The Pittsburgh Conference had envisaged no return to Palestine and had insisted that the Jews did not constitute a nation. The Union of American Hebrew Congregations proclaimed, "America is our Zion," and the Central Conference of American Rabbis in 1896 and '97 and again in 1912 and '17 had specifically condemned the Zionist program. The Yiddishist labor movement was also generally hostile. To the Orthodox, moreover, the dispersion had a religious significance and was not to be terminated by human political measures. In a very broad sense, the immigrants had made their choice of a promised land when they came to America, and Palestine did not loom very large in their consciousness.
>
> There was a romantic attachment to the biblical scene that turned the minds of such people as Mordecai M. Noah, Emma Lazarus and Henrietta Szold to Palestine. But, significantly, the latter were not immigrants, being rather natives, and imbued with American ideas. The newcomers were too concerned with their own problems of settlement to give much thought to another homeland. Consequently, although traditional connections with Palestine were maintained through messengers and relief funds, the Federation of American Zionists had only 8,000 members in the United States in 1900.
>
> The first World War and its aftermath marked the first turning point. Americans were then elevated to the leadership of world Jewry and played a prominent part in the peace conferences. The Balfour Declaration and the mandate made some sort of Jewish homeland in Palestine a reality. At the same time, unsettled condi-

tions in Europe and the closing of the American gates left large groups of European Jews with whom the recent American immigrants had close familial ties anxious to move but with no place to go. The number of Americans who showed their adherence to the Zionist program by purchasing a shekel mounted from 20,000 in 1914 to 170,000 in 1920. Even the Reform Central Conference of American Rabbis, though still opposed to a Jewish state, came out in favor of immigration to Palestine in 1918 on the ground that "Jewish people are, and of right ought to be, at home in all lands." The growth of American Zionist sentiment marked by revival of interest in the Hebrew language and by cooperation with Palestinian social and economic development was steady in the 1920's.

Here too, Hitlerism forced the decisive division, induced the Jewish labor movement to espouse Zionism, pushed the Reform wing of Judaism into a position of official neutrality and unofficial support, and strengthened Orthodox approval. By 1945, American Jews stood almost solidly behind the Zionists. Nazism made enormous numbers of Jews homeless and callous restrictions in every other part of the world left Palestine the sole haven. The shock of discovering how small a proportion of Europe's Jews actually survived the decade of fanaticism and war made the task of rescuing the remnant all the more urgent.

But the enormous increase of interest in Zionism was also a result of conditions in the United States. As in the case of other immigrant groups, political nationalism offered a temporary release from the fears and frustrations incidental to adjustment. For here was a way of escaping from the harshness of contact with strangers, a way of finding security in affiliation with the ethnic group, yet a way that was acceptable in terms of the standards of the larger society. The Jews behaved as the Irish and Germans had done earlier; feeling rejected by the "100 per cent Americans," they turned to a similar nationalism of their own. Zionism was the outlet, particularly for the second generation Jews, perplexed as all second generations were by the question of their place in American culture, confused by their own specifically Jewish problems of social and economic adjustment, and anxious over the meaning of anti-Semitism. Americans were extremists in the world Zionist movement, in a small measure because they carried into it the whole burden of their worries and fears as American Jews.[1]

The Zionist commitment of American Jews played an important role in the recovery of self-respect and a stable community life. Long before the establishment of the State of Israel, Milton Steinberg described both the effects of the Zionist enterprise on Jews of his time,

[1] Oscar and Mary F. Handlin, "A Century of Jewish Immigration to the United States," *The American Jewish Yearbook,* L (1948–1949), 78–80.

and the future impact of the Jewish State on world Jewry. It should be clear that Steinberg's case is addressed to the American Jewish situation: Zionism is important at home, and to Judaism; the "Jewish homeland" will change *American* Jews.

That Zionism has pertinence for American Jews, the more perceptive American Zionists are keenly aware. They know full well that their program reflects self-interest as well as philanthropy. Deep within them and their group existence are ills that can be remedied, and lacks that can be supplied only by a Jewish National Home.

Or to put it otherwise, they sense that while Palestine is a necessity for the bodies of other Jews, it is an indispensability for their own souls. With it they have a better than fair chance of maintaining their religion and culture, and of bringing both to heightened self-realization. Without it the future is much less encouraging. Indeed, it is not unlikely that the fate of Judaism in the New World may be decided, for weal or for woe, by the outcome of an experiment some six thousand miles removed.

This is not to say that a Jewish Homeland will, of and by itself, resolve any of the many problems of American Jewry. Jewish theology has never supported the doctrine of vicarious salvation. No one, rabbis and sages hold, can be saved by anyone else; in the end each man must redeem his own soul. Yet in the quest for redemption, one can be helped or hindered, sometimes decisively, by external influences.

So with American Jews in their relation to Palestine. Theirs is the difficult but inescapable task of disposing creatively of problems, theological, ritual, ethical, cultural and organizational. Yet in it they can be strengthened or disheartened by forces from without. Jewish Palestine is already a constructive influence in their lives. It gives promise of playing an even larger role in the future. It may well prove to be decisive between survival and extinction.

How then is a Jewish Homeland in Palestine likely to make American Jews stronger and better as human beings, richer and more resolute in their Judaism? . . .

. . . the fulfillment of the Zionist program may normalize Jews in the eyes of the world. As matters now stand, Jews are indeed a "peculiar" people. They are in so many respects *sui generis*. They are a religious communion, and yet something more; a culture group, but not that exclusively; a people, but lacking what all other peoples possess—a Homeland. This quality of the abnormal, the idiosyncratic, may have made no slight contribution to the extraordinary position of the Jews in general esteem. Men tend to be puzzled by and resentful of the unusual and the unprecedented.

Let a Jewish Commonwealth be set up in Palestine, and the aura of the eccentric will be dissipated. Palestine Jewry will certainly constitute a normal sociological and psychological phenomenon, one more of all the peoples rooted in their own soil. Jews in the Diaspora may also take on a new aspect. Like Swedish, Irish or Italian Americans, they may come to be regarded as persons who, though descendants of a people with a land of its own, have elected America for their country and home. Divested of qualities of the bizarre, almost the spectral, they may be accepted more conventionally.

These are possibilities, conjectures as to the impact of Zionism on the social status of American Jewry. Of one other consequence it is possible to speak with greater assurance.

Palestine can help American Jews by mitigating anti-Semitism in those lands that heretofore have been its chief breeding grounds. Prejudice against Jews has for centuries been endemic and fierce in Central Europe. Out of this focal point of infection the virus has seeped again and again to poison the world. Zionism, by draining off a substantial part of the Jews of the diseased areas, will ease long-sustained pressures. The inflammation will subside most immediately at its center, but subsequently throughout the whole organism of society. Badly stated: Let 2,000,000 Jews move from Europe to Palestine, and there will be improvement in the lot of Jews everywhere.

Consider, for example, the problem of Jewish morale, that distressing and dangerous tendency of the Jewish personality to slip into self-contempt and self-repudiation. In no respect does Zionism serve the American Jew so signally as in inoculating him against such psychic perils.

In the first place, Zionism represents one of the few Jewish activities that are inherently positive and creative in character. It is difficult for a non-Jew ignorant of the Jewish scene, it is next to impossible for a Jew close to it, to discern how much of what passes for Jewish enterprise is negative and sterile.

In their specifically Jewish self-expression, American Jews expend most of their energy on self-defense and philanthropy. Both of these are necessary; neither is inherently worth while. That is to say, no person of good will would wish for the continuance of anti-Semitism so that Jews may have occasion to go on combating it, or for the persistence of indigence, insanity, orphanhood and senility just in order that Jews may be compelled to maintain charitable institutions. In consequence, the American Jewish community is much like a beseiged hospital. Its denizens are very busy repelling attacks and taking care of the unfortunate, but have much too little to do with sanctuaries and libraries, with the experiences that redeem effort from emptiness and futility.

Men have long known the truth of which James and Lange made a proposition: that, while our actions reflect our feelings, our feelings mirror our behavior. Generally we are first happy and then smile, or first afraid and then run away, but not infrequently the reverse is the case. We run long enough and begin to feel afraid, or force ourselves to smile and end by feeling happy. In other words, what a man *does* about anything has a great deal to do with how he will *feel* about it.

Now, as we have just noted, most of what most American Jews do, *qua* Jews, is negative. A mood is engendered. They begin to feel the way they behave. To be forever repelling attacks by anti-Semites is a weariness of the flesh and vexation of the spirit. To spend one's Jewish existence in the atmosphere of a relief agency or a hospital means that Judaism comes to smell of ether and to suggest the miseries to which the flesh is heir. Neither development favors self-respect or a keen desire to live Jewishly.

Among the handful of Jewish causes that are not woebegone, Palestine is one, perhaps the most conspicuous. It seeks to incarnate an ancient dream, to establish a cultural center for world Jewry, to realize the peoplehood of Israel, all positive objectives, all purposes that would be pursued were there not a single Jew-baiter or baited Jew on earth. To this program, anti-Semitism has given an extra edge, but as a matter of accident, not essence, as something thrown in for bad measure by the caprice of history.

And because Zionism has worth in its own right, because it is cheerful, it makes a major contribution to the spirit of American Jews. As the Zionist exerts himself for Jewish ends to which his heart can say "Amen," there are distilled in him self-acceptance and confidence in the value of Judaism and the Jewish identity, the prerequisites for psychic health. Not that Zionism is alone in exerting a benign influence on the Jewish personality; Jewish religion, ethic, ritual and culture when properly cultivated have the same effect. But in the catalogue of counteragents to Jewish self-contempt, this item stands very high and looms very large.

Louis Adamic in *From Many Lands* relates how American Finns, exhibiting all the insecurities of a minority group, were psychically reassured by the very existence of Sibelius; how American Greeks in a similar pass were made the more self-confident by the heroic resistance put up by other Greeks in their native land. So with the American Jew, Palestine cannot do the whole job for him, but it can and does help.

Towering above all else is the fact that Jewish Palestine has evoked a renaissance of Jewish culture, that the Judaism of every Jew throughout the world is the richer therefor, that his will to be a Jew is thereby enhanced. Herein consists the greatest contribution of Zionism to American Jewish morale.

This is the final gift of Jewish Palestine to American Judaism —a gift larger than all contributions to social status or culture— the gift of *elan*, hopefulness, a conviction of worth, in sum, a confidence in the future of Israel [the Jewish people] and its way of life.[2]

---

[2] Steinberg, *A Partisan Guide to the Jewish Problem*, pp. 267–68, 269–70, 270–72, 272–73, 278.

Now, nearly a quarter of a century after the establishment of the State of Israel, the results are in. Zionism has done what Steinberg claimed it would—in a way. This writer has suggested how Zionism has done away with "the Jewish problem" which it to begin with defined and determined to solve.

When Herzl proposed Zionism as the solution to the Jewish problem, the "Zionism" of which he spoke and the "Jewish problem" which he proposed to solve constituted chiefly political realities. But, as Arthur Hertzberg trenchantly argues in *The Zionist Idea,* Zionism actually represented not a merely secular and political ideology, but the transvaluation of Jewish values. If so, the same must be said of the "Jewish problem" to which it addresses itself. Zionism as an external force faced the world, but what shall we say of its inner spirit? The inwardness of Zionism—its "piety" and spirituality—is not to be comprehended by the world, only by the Jew, for, like the Judaism it transformed and transcended, to the world it was worldly and political, stiff-necked and stubborn (in Christian theological terms), but to the Jew it was something other, not to be comprehended by the gentile. . . .

The Zionism of which I speak is the effort to realize through political means the hope supposed to have been lost in the time of Ezekiel, proclaimed imperishable in the time of Imber, the continuous hope of restoration and renaissance first of the land of Israel, then of the people of Israel through the land, finally, since 1948, of the people and the land together, wherever the people should be found. This Zionism did not come about at Basel, for its roots go back to the point in the ages at which Jewry first recognized, then rejected, its separation from the land. Zionism is the old-new Judaism, a Judaism transformed through old-new values. It is a set of paradoxes through which the secular and the religious, separated in the nineteenth century, were again fused— re-fused—in the twentieth. Zionism to be sure is a complex phenomenon; within it are tendencies which are apt to cancel each other. But all forms of Zionism are subsumed under the definition offered here, which represents, I think, the lowest common denominator for all Zionist phenomena.

The Jewish problems which Zionism successfully solved were the consequences of the disintegration of what had been whole, the identity, consciousness, and the culture of the Jew. It was, as I said, Zionism which reconstructed the whole and reshaped the tradition in a wholly new heuristic framework.

In former times it was conventional to speak of the "Jewish problem." Most people understood that problem in political and economic terms. What shall we do about the vast Jewish populations of Eastern and Central Europe, which live a marginal economic life and have no place in the political structures of the several nations? Herzl proposed the Zionist solution to the "Jewish problem." Dubnow wished to solve the "Jewish problem" by the creation of Jewish autonomous units in Europe. The Socialists and Communists proposed to solve the "Jewish problem" by the integration of Jewry into the movement of the international proletariat and to complete the solution of the problems of the smaller group within those of the working classes.

Today we hear less talk about the "Jewish problem" because Hitler brought it to a final solution: By exterminating the masses of European Jews, he left unsolved no social, economic, or political problems. The Western Jewries are more or less well-integrated into the democratic societies. The State of Israel has no "Jewish problem" in the classic sense. The oppressed communities remaining in the Arab countries are relatively small, and the solution of their problems is to be found in migration to the West and to the State of Israel. The "Jewish problem" to be sure continues to confront Soviet Russia, and there the classic Marxist formulation of the problem still persuades people. But, for the rest, the "Jewish problem" does not describe reality or evoke a recognized, real-life perplexity. (That does not mean Jews do not have problems, or that gentiles do not have problems in relating to and understanding both Jews and Judaism.)

I shall concentrate on three aspects of the contemporary Jewish situation, all closely related, and all the result of secularism. The first is the crisis of identity, the second, the liberal dilemma, the third, the problem of self-hatred. The Jewish identity-crisis may be simply stated: There is no consensus shared by most Jews about what a Jew is, how Judaism should be defined, what "being Jewish" and "Judaism" are supposed to mean for individuals and the community. The liberal dilemma is this: How can I espouse universal principles and yet remain part of a particular community? The problem of self-hatred needs little definition, but provokes much illustration, for many of the phenomena of contemporary Jewish life reflect the low self-esteem attached to being Jewish.

The secular revolution has imposed upon Jews a profound crisis of identity. In former times everyone knew who was a Jew and what being a Jew meant. A Jew was a member of a religious nation, living among other nations by its own laws, believing in *Torah* revealed at Sinai and in one God who had chosen Israel, and hoping for the coming of the Messiah. The gentile world shared the philosophical presuppositions of Jewish beliefs. Everyone believed in God. Everyone believed in prophecy, in revelation, in the Jews' holy book. Everyone believed in the coming of the Messiah. Above all, everyone interpreted reality by supernaturalist principles. To be sure groups differed on the nature of God, the particular prophets to be regarded as true, the book God had revealed. But these differences took place within a vast range of agreement.

When religious understandings of the world lost their hold on masses of Western men, "being Jewish" became as problematical as any other aspect of archaic reality. If to be Jewish meant to be part of a Jewish religious community, then when men ceased to believe in religious propositions, they ought to have ceased being Jewish. Yet that is not what happened. For several generations Jewish atheists and agnostics have continued to take an active role in the Jewish community—indeed, functionally to constitute the majority in it—and to have seen nothing unusual either in their participation in Jewish life or in their lack of religious commitment. Indeed today the American Jewish community is nearly unique in interpreting "being Jewish" primarily in religious, or at least rhetorically religious, terms. Other Jewish communities see themselves as a community, a nation, a people, whether or not religion plays a role in defining what is particular about that community. The secular revolution immensely complicated the definition of Jewish identity, not only by breaking down the uniform classical definition, but also by supplying a variety of new, complex definitions in its place.

Today, therefore, if we ask ourselves, "What are the components of 'Jewishness'?" we are hard put to find an answer. What are the attitudes, associations, rituals both secular and religious, psychology and culture, which both Jews and others conceive to be Jewish? The truth is, today there is no such thing as a single Jewish identity, as there assuredly was in times past an identity one could define in meaningful terms. Jewishness now is a function of various social and cultural settings, and is meaningful in those settings only.

The Jews obviously are not a nation in the accepted sense; but they also are hardly a people in the sense that an outsider can investigate or understand the components of that peoplehood. There is no "Jewish way" of organizing experience and interpreting reality, although there was and is a Judaic way. There is no single Jewish ideology, indeed no single, unitary "Jewish history," although there once was a cogent Judaic theology and a Judaic view of a unitary and meaningful progression of events to be called "Jewish history." Only if we impose upon discrete events of scarcely related groups in widely separated places and ages the concept of a single unitary history can we speak of "Jewish history." Jewish peoplehood in a concrete, secular, this-worldly historical sense is largely a matter of faith, that is, the construction of historians acting as do theologians in other settings. There once was a single Jewish ideological system, a coherent body of shared images, ideas and ideals, which provided for participants a coherent over-all orientation in space and time, in means and ends. There once was such a system, but in the secular revolution it has collapsed.

. . . the secular revolution . . . imposed on Jewry a lingering crisis of identity. Jews today may find in common a set of emotions and responses. These do not constitute an "identity," but rather, . . . common characteristics based upon differing verbal explanations and experiences. That does not mean no one knows what a Jew is. In particular settings Jews *can* be defined and understood in terms applicable to those settings. But as an abstraction the "Jewish people" is a theological or ideological construct not to be imposed upon the disparate, discrete data known as Jews or even as Jewish communities in various times and places. Lacking a common language and culture, even a common religion, the Jews do not have what they once had. Today Jewish identity so greatly varies that we need to reconsider the viability of the very concept of "Jewishness" as a universal attribute, for today Jewishness cannot be defined in neutral, cultural terms.

If there are no inherent and essential Jewish qualities in the world, then nothing about "being Jewish" is natural, to be taken for granted. Being Jewish becomes something one must achieve, define, strive for. It is today liberated from the forms and content of the recent past, from the "culture-Judaism" of the American and Canadian Jewish communities. If the artifacts of that "culture-Judaism"—matters of cuisine, or philanthropy, or cliquishness— are not part of some immutable and universal Jewish identity, then they may well be criticized from within, not merely abandoned and left behind in disgust. One can freely repudiate them in favor of other ways.

Omissions in contemporary Jewish "identity" are as striking as the inclusions. Among the things taken for granted are a sense of group-loyalty, a desire to transmit "pride in Judaism" to the next generation, in all a desire to survive. But the identity of large numbers of Jews, whether they regard themselves as secular or not, does not include a concept of God, of the meaning of life, of the direction and purpose of history. The uncriticized, but widely accepted Jewish-identity syndrome is formed of the remnants of the piety of the recent past, a piety one may best call residual, cultural, and habitual, rather than self-conscious, critical, and theological (or ideological). That identity is not even ethnic, but rather a conglomeration of traits picked up in particular historical and social experiences. It is certainly flat and one-dimensional, leaving Jews to wander in strange paths in search of the answers to the most fundamental human perplexities.

Why are Jews in the forefront of universal causes, to the exclusion of their own interest and identity? Charles Liebman, writing in *The Religious Situation 1969,* examines the reasons given for this phenomenon. He rejects the notion that Jewish liberalism, cosmopolitanism, and internationalism rest on "traditional" Jewish values, for, he points out, it is the secular, not the religious, Jew who espouses cosmopolitanism. Jewish religious values in fact are folk-oriented rather than universalistic.

Liebman likewise rejects the view that the Jews' social status, far below what they might anticipate from their economic attainments, accounts for their attraction to the fringes of politics. This theory accounts, Liebman says, for Jewish radicalism rather than Jewish liberalism, that is, for only a small element of the community. Further, Jewish radicals normally abandon Jewish community life; the liberals dominate it.

A third explanation derives from the facts of history. Liberal parties supported the emancipation of the Jews; conservative ones opposed it. But for the U.S.A. this was not the case. Indeed, until the New Deal, Jews tended to be Republican, not Democratic or Socialist. Liebman posits that the appeal of liberalism is among Jews estranged from the religious tradition. This appeal, he says, "lies in the search for a universalistic ethic to which a Jew can adhere *but* which is seemingly irrelevant to specific Jewish concerns and, unlike radical socialism, does not demand total commitment at the expense of all other values."

Since the Emancipation, Jews have constantly striven to free themselves from the condition which Judaism thrusts on them. This Liebman calls estrangement: "The impetus for intellectual and religious reform among Jews, the adoption of new ideologies and life styles, but above all else the changing self-perception by the Jew of himself and his condition was not simply a desire to find amelioration from the physical oppression of the ghetto. It was rather a desire for emancipation from the very essence of the Jewish condition. . . . The Jew's problem was his alienation from the roots and the traditions of the society."

Here is the point at which the phenomenon of secularization becomes important. Jews earlier knew they were different, estranged. But with the collapse of religious evaluation of that difference, the Jews ceased to affirm their particularity. Secularization changed the nature of the Jew's perception of his condition, transferred the estrangement from theology to the realm of contemporary culture and civilization.

Jews supported universal humanism and cosmopolitanism with a vengeance. They brought these ideals home to the community so that Jewish difference was played down. Look, for example, at the Union Prayerbook, and count the number of times the congregation prays for "all mankind." The New Liberal Prayerbook in England so emphasizes the universal to the exclusion of the particular that one might write to the English liberal rabbi responsible for the liturgy: "Warm and affectionate regards to your wife and children, and to all mankind." Liebman concludes, "The Jew wished to be accepted as an equal in society *not* because he was a Jew, but because his Jewishness was *irrelevant.* Yet at the same time, the Jew refused to make his own Jewishness irrelevant. . . . He made . . . contradictory demands on society. He wants to be accepted into the tradition of society without adapting to the society's dominant tradition." This constitutes the liberal dilemma: how to affirm universalism and remain particular.

Complex though is the liberal identity of secular Jews, it is still more complicated by the phenomena of anti-Semitism and consequent self-hatred. The "Jewish problem" is most commonly phrased by young Jews as "Why should I be Jewish? I believe in universal ideals—who needs particular ones as well?"

Minorities feel themselves "particular," see their traditions as "ritual," and distinguish between the private, unique, and personal and the public, universal, and commonplace. Majorities do not. Standing at the center, not on the fringe, they accept the given. Marginal men such as the Jews regard the given as something to be be criticized, elevated, in any event as distinguished from their own essential being.

Jews who ask, "Why be Jewish," testify that "being Jewish" somehow repels, separates a person from the things he wants. American society, though it is opening, still is not so open that men who are different from the majority can serenely and happily accept that difference. True, they frequently affirm it—but the affirmation contains such excessive protest that it is not much different from denial. The quintessential datum of American Jewish existence is anti-Semitism, along with uncertainty of status, denial of normality, and self-doubt. The results are many, but two stand out. Some overemphasize their Jewishness, respond to it not naturally but excessively, to the exclusion of other parts of their being. Others question and implicitly deny it. The one compensates too much; the other finds no reward at all.

As Kurt Lewin pointed out ". . . every underprivileged minority group is kept together not only by cohesive forces among its members but also by the boundary which the majority erects against the crossing of an individual from the minority to the majority group." [3] An underprivileged group-member will try to gain in social status by joining the majority—to pass, to assimilate. The basic fact of life is this wish to cross the boundary, and hence, as Lewin says, "he [the minority-group member] lives almost perpetually in a state of conflict and tension. He dislikes . . . his own group because it is nothing but a burden to him. . . . A Jew of this type will dislike everything specifically Jewish, for he will see in it that which keeps him away from the majority for which he is longing." Such a Jew is the one who will constantly ask, "Why be Jewish?" who will see, or at least fantasize about, a common religion of humanity, universalism or universal values that transcend, and incidentally obliterate, denominational and sectarian

[3] Kurt Lewin, *Resolving Social Conflicts, Selected Papers on Group Dynamics* (New York: Harper and Row, Publishers, 1948), p. 164.

boundaries. It is no accident that the universal language, Esperanto, the universal movement, Communism, and the universal psychology, Freudianism, all were in large measure attractive to marginal Jews.

True, Jews may find a place in social groups indifferent to their particularity as Jews. But a closer look shows that these groups are formed chiefly by deracinated, de-Judaised Jews, along with a few exceptionally liberal non-Jews standing in a similar relationship to their own origins. Jews do assimilate. They do try to blot out the marks of their particularity, in ways more sophisticated, to be sure, than the ancient Hellenist-Jews who submitted to painful operations to wipe away the marks of circumcision. But in doing so, they become not something else entirely, but another type of Jew. The real issue is never, to be or not to be a Jew, any more than it is, to be or not to be my father's son.

Lewin makes this wholly clear: "It is not similarity or dissimilarity of individuals that constitutes a group, but interdependence of fate." Jews brought up to suppose being Jewish is chiefly, or only, a matter of religion think that through atheism they cease to be Jews, only to discover that disbelieving in God helps not at all. They still are Jews. They still are obsessed by that fact and compelled to confront it, whether under the name of Warren or of Weinstein, whether within the society of Jews or elsewhere.

Indeed, outside of that society Jewish consciousness becomes most intense. Among Jews one is a human being, with peculiarities and virtues of one's own. Among gentiles he is a Jew, with traits common to the group he rejects. That is probably why Jews still live in mostly Jewish neighborhoods and associate, outside of economic life, mostly with other Jews, whether or not these associations exhibit traits supposed to be Jewish. And when crisis comes, as it frequently does, then no one doubts that he shares a common cause, a common fate, with other Jews. Then it is hardest to isolate oneself from Jews, because only among Jewry are these intense concerns shared.

What has Zionism to do with these Jewish problems? It is, after all, supposedly a secular movement, called "secular messianism," and the problems I have described are the consequences of secularity. How then has an allegedly secular movement posited solutions to the challenges of secularity faced by the formerly religious community?

Zionism provides a reconstruction of Jewish identity, for it reaffirms the nationhood of Israel in the face of the disintegration of the religious bases of Jewish peoplehood. If in times past the Jews saw themselves as a people because they were the children of the promise, the children of Abraham, Isaac, and Jacob, called together at Sinai, instructed by God through prophets, led by rabbis guided by the "whole Torah"—written and oral—of Sinai, then with the end of a singularly religious self-consciousness, the people lost its understanding of itself. The fact is that the people remained a community of fate, but, until the flourishing of Zionism, the facts of its continued existence were deprived of a heuristic foundation. Jews continued as a group, but could not persuasively say why or what this meant. Zionism provided the explanation: The Jews indeed remain a people, but the foundation of their peoplehood lies in the unity of their concern for Zion, devotion to rebuilding the land and establishing Jewish sovereignty in it. The realities of continuing emotional and social commitment to Jewish "grouphood" or separateness thus made sense. Mere secular difference, once seen to be destiny—"who has not made us like the nations"— once again stood forth as destiny.

Herein lies the ambiguity of Zionism. It was supposedly a secular movement, yet in reinterpreting the classic mythic structures of Judaism, it compromised its secularity and exposed its fundamental unity with the classic mythic being of Judaism. If, as I suggested, groups with like attributes do not necessarily represent "peoples" or "nations," and if the common attributes, in the Jewish case, are neither intrinsically Jewish (whatever that might mean) nor widely present to begin with, then the primary conviction of Zionism constitutes an extraordinary reaffirmation of the primary element in the classical mythic structure: salvation. What has happened in Zionism is that the old has been in one instant destroyed and resurrected. The "holy people" are no more, the nation-people take their place. How much has changed in the religious tradition, when the allegedly secular successor-continuator has preserved not only the essential perspective of the tradition, but done so pretty much in the tradition's own symbols and language?

Nor should it be supposed that the Zionist solution to the Jews' crisis of identity is a merely theological or ideological one. We cannot ignore the practical result of Zionist success in conquering the Jewish community. For the middle and older generations, as everyone knows, the Zionist enterprise provided the primary vehicle for Jewish identity. The Reform solution to the identity-problem —we are Americans by nationality, Jews by religion—was hardly congruent to the profound Jewish passion of the immigrant generations and their children. The former generations were *not* merely Jewish by religion. Religion was the least important aspect of their Jewishness. They deeply felt themselves Jewish in their bone and marrow and did not feel sufficiently marginal as Jews to *need* to affirm their Americanness/Judaism at all. Rather they participated in a reality; they were in a situation so real and intimate as to make unnecessary such an uncomfortable, defensive affirmation. They did not doubt they were Americans. They did not need to explain what being Jewish had to do with it. Zionism was congruent to these realities, and because of that fact, being Jewish and being Zionist were inextricably joined together.

The Zionist critique of the Jews' liberal dilemma is no less apt. Zionism has not stood against liberal causes and issues. On the contrary, Zionist Socialists have stood at the forefront of the liberal cause, have struggled for the working-class ideals, have identified the working class cause with their own. The record of Israeli and American Zionist thought on liberal issues is unambiguous and consistent. The liberalism of which Liebman writes is of a different order. It is a liberalism not born in Jewish nationhood but despite and against it. The liberal cosmopolitan Jew, devoted to internationalism and universal causes to the exclusion of "parochial" Jewish concerns, is no Zionist, but the opposite. He is a Jew acting out the consequences of deracination in the political arena. His universal liberalism takes the place of a profound commitment to the Jews and their welfare. Indeed, it is a liberalism that would like to deny that Jews have special, particular interests and needs to begin with. "Struggling humanity" in all its forms but one claim his sympathy: when Jews suffer, they *have* to do so as part of undifferentiated humanity.

So far as this Jewish liberalism was non-sectarian and hostile to the things that concern Jews as Jews—as in those Jewish welfare federations which articulately state their purpose as humanitarian to the exclusion of Judaism—Zionism has rejected that liberalism. It has done so because of its critical view of the Emancipation. Unlike the Jewish liberals, the Zionist saw the Emancipation as a problem, not a solution. He was dubious of its promises and aware of its hypocrisies. He saw Emancipation as a threat to Jewry and in slight measure a benefit for Jews. The Jews' problem was that Emancipation represented de-Judaization. The price of admission to the roots and traditions of "society" was the surrender of the roots and traditions of the Jew, so said Zionist thought.

At the same time the Zionist stood between the religious party, which utterly rejected Emancipation and its works, and the secular-reform-liberal party, which wholly affirmed them. He faced the reality of Emancipation without claiming in its behalf a messianic valence. Emancipation is here, he thought, therefore to be criticized, but coped with; not utterly rejected, like the Orthodox, no wholeheartedly affirmed, like the secular, reform and liberal groups. Zionism therefore demanded that the Jew be accepted as an equal in society because he was a Jew, *not* because his Jewishness was irrelevant. Its suspicion of the liberal stance was based, correctly in my opinion, on the Jews' ambivalence toward Jewishness. Zionism clearly recognized that the Jewishness of the Jew could never be irrelevant, not to the gentile, not to the Jew. It therefore saw more clearly than the liberals the failures of the European Emancipation and the dangers of American liberalism to Jewish self-respect and Jewish interests. Zionists were quick to perceive the readiness of non-Jewish allies of Jewish liberals to take the Jewish liberals at their word: We Jews have no special interests, nothing to fight for in our own behalf. Zionists saw Jews had considerable interests, just like other groups, and exposed the self-deceit (or hypocrisy) of those who said otherwise. The liberal Jew wanted to be accepted into the traditions of society without complete assimilation, on the one side, but also without much Jewishness, on the other. The Zionist assessment of the situation differed, as I said, for it saw that Jews could achieve a place in the common life *only* as Jews; and, rightly for Europe, it held this was impossible.

In its gloomy assessment of the European Emancipation, Zionism found itself in a position to cope with the third component in the Jewish problem, the immense, deep-rooted, and wide-ranging self-hatred of Jews. The Zionist affirmation of Jewish peoplehood, of Jewish-being, stood in stark contrast to the inability of marginal and liberal Jews to cope with anti-Semitism. Cases too numerous to list demonstrate the therapeutic impact of Zionism on the faltering psychological health of European Jews, particularly of more sensitive and intellectual individuals.

The American situation is different in degree, for here anti-Semitism in recent times has made its impact in more subtle ways, but its presence is best attested by the Jews themselves. Yet if a single factor in the self-respect American Jewry does possess can be isolated, it is its pride in the State of Israel and its achievements. Zionism lies at the foundation of American Jewry's capacity to affirm its Jewishness. Without Zionism, religious conviction, forced to bear the whole burden by itself, would prove a slender reed. To be a Jew "by religion" and to make much of that fact in an increasingly secular environment would not represent an attractive option to many. The contributions to Jewry's psychological health by the State of Israel and the Zionist presence in the Diaspora cannot be over-estimated. It is striking, for example, that Kurt Lewin, Milton Steinberg, and other students of the phenomenon of Jewish self-hatred invariably reached the single conclusion that only through Zionism would self-hatred be mitigated, even overcome.

The role of Zionism as a therapy for self-hatred cannot be described only in terms of the public opinion of U.S. Jewry. That would tell us much about the impact of mass communications, but little about the specific value of the Zionist idea for healing the Jewish pathology. In my view, the Israelis' claim "to live a full Jewish life" is a valid one. In Zionist conception and Israeli reality, the Jew is indeed a thoroughly integrated, whole human being. Here, in conception and reality, the Jew who believes in justice, truth, and peace, in universal brotherhood and dignity, does so not despite his peculiarity as a Jew, but through it. He makes no distinction between his Jewishness, his humanity, his individuality, his way of living, and his ultimate values. They constitute a single, undivided and fully integrated existential reality.

Part of the reason is the condition of life: The State of Israel is the largest Jewish neighborhood in the world. But part of the reason is ideological, and not merely circumstantial: Zionists always have rejected the possibility of Jews' "humanity" without Jewishness, just as they denied the reality of distinctions between Jewishness, nationality, and faith. They were not only *not* Germans of the Mosaic persuasions, but also *not* human beings of the Jewish genus. The several sorts of bifurcations attempted by non-Zionists to account for their Jewishness along with other sorts of putatively non-Jewish commitments and loyalties were rejected by Zionists. It was not that Zionists did not comprehend the dilemmas faced by other sorts of Jews, but rather that they supposed through Zionism they had found the solution. They correctly held that through Zionist ideology and activity they had overcome the disintegrating Jewish identity-crisis of others.

At the outset I suggested that, like Judaism, Zionism can be understood from within, from its soul. My claim is that Zionism is to be understood as a solution to Jewish problems best perceived by the Jews who face those problems. The "Jewish problem" imposed by the effects of secularism took the form of a severe and complex crisis of identity, a partial commitment to universalism and cosmopolitan liberalism while claiming the right to be a little different, and a severe psycho-pathological epidemic of self-hatred. But the way Zionism actually solved those problems is more difficult to explain. If, as I suppose, because of Zionism contemporary Jewries have a clearer perception of who they are, what their interests consist of, and of their value as human beings, then Zionism and the State of Israel are in substantial measure the source of the "saving knowledge." But *how* has Zionism worked its salvation on the Jews? Here I think we come to realities only Jews can understand. They understand them *not* because of rational reflection but because of experience and unreflective, natural response.

Zionism, and Zionism alone, proved capable of interpreting to contemporary Jews the meaning of felt-history, *and* of doing so in terms congruent to what the Jews derived from their tradition. It was Zionism which properly assessed the limitations of the Emancipation and proposed sound and practical programs to cope with those limitations. It was Zionism which gave Jews strength to affirm themselves when faced with the anti-Semitism of European and American life in the first-half of the twentieth century. It was Zionism and that alone which showed a way forward from the nihilism and despair of the DP camps. It was Zionism and that alone which provided a basis for unity in U.S. Jewry in the fifties and sixties of this century, a ground for common action among otherwise utterly divided groups.

These achievements of Zionism were based not on their practicality, though Zionism time and again was proved "right" by history. The Jews were moved and responded to Zionism before, not after the fact. And they were moved because of the capacity of Zionism to resurrect the single most powerful force in the history of Judaism: Messianism. Zionism did so in ways too numerous to list, but the central fact is that it represented, as Hertzberg perceptively showed, not "secular Messianism" but a profound restatement in new ways of classical Messianism. Zionism recovered the old, still evocative messianic symbolism and imagery and filled them with new meaning. And *this* meaning was taken for granted by vast numbers of Jews because it accurately described not what they believed or hoped for—not faith—but rather what they took to be mundane reality. Zionism took within its heuristic framework each and every important event in twentieth-century Jewish history and gave to all a single, comprehensive, and sensible interpretation. Events were no longer random or unrelated, but all were part of a single pattern, pointing toward an attainable messianic result. It was not the random degradation of individuals in Germany and Poland, not the meaningless murder of unfortunates, not the creation of another state in the Middle East. All of these events were related to one another. It was Holocaust and rebirth, and the state was the State of *Israel*.

In so stating the meaning of contemporary events, Zionism made it possible for Jews not only to understand what they witnessed, but to draw meaning from it. And even more, Zionism breathed new life into ancient Scriptures, by providing a contemporary interpretation—subtle and not fundamentalist to be sure—for the prophets. "Our hope is lost," Ezekiel denied in the name of God. "Our hope is not lost," was the response of Zionism. These things were no accident, still less the result of an exceptionally clever publicist's imagination. They demonstrate the center and core of Zionist spirituality and piety: the old-new myth of peoplehood, land, redemption above all. The astonishing achievements of Zionism are the result of the capacity of Zionism to reintegrate the tradition with contemporary reality, to do so in an entirely factual, matter-of-fact framework, thus to eschew faith and to elicit credence. Zionism speaks in terms of Judaic myth, indeed so profundly that myth and reality coincide.[4]

On the other hand, Zionism posed serious dilemmas to the classic Judaic tradition in its contemporary formulation. In many ways the success of Zionism, in bringing to a happy conclusion some of the problems faced by modern Jews, has produced the opposite of a secular and modern effect. It has pointed up those aspects of human life left untouched by modernity. The most modern and secular side of contemporary Judaism once again focuses attention upon the archaic and

---

[4] Jacob Neusner, "Zionism and 'The Jewish Problem,'" *Midstream*, XV, No. 9 (November, 1969), 34–45.

religious, for the mythic insufficiency of Zionism directs contemporary Jews to other aspects of the classical forms of Judaism.

The success of Zionism in solving the central Jewish problems of the modern age also creates new dilemmas for the Judaic religious tradition. Since Zionism functions for Jewry in much the same way as religions do for other peoples, the role and function of *Judaism* —the complex of myths, rituals, social and cultural forms by which classical Jews experienced and interpreted reality—now prove exceptionally ambiguous. Because Zionism appropriates the eschatological language and symbolism of classical Judaism, Judaists face an unwanted alternative: either to repudiate Zionism or to acquiesce in the historicization, the politicization, of what had formerly stood above politics and beyond history. The choice to be sure was recognized and faced by small reform and orthodox circles, as everyone knows. The classical reformers repudiated Zionism in the name of the mission of Israel, which, they held, required Jewry to take a decisive role in the universal achievement by all men of the Messianic age. Their last, and unworthy, heirs accurately repeat the rhetoric, but do not possess the moral authority, of the nineteenth-century reformers. Likewise, orthodox leadership in Eastern Europe and the U. S. A. quite early discerned what they understood to be the heretical tendency of Zionism: the advocacy that Jews save themselves, rather than depend on the Messiah, and return to Zion before the foreordained end of time. Their repulsive continuators present no interesting differences from the anti-Zionist reformers.

For the great mass of American Jews, who take literally the Zionist interpretation of Jewish history and innocently identify Zionism with Judaism, but regard themselves also both as Americans by nationality and Jews by religion, naive belief substitutes for and precludes close analysis. They have yet to come to grips with the inner contradictions recognized by the extremists of reform and orthodox Judaism. Indeed, they exasperate Israeli Zionists as much as Diaspora anti-Zionists. If Zionist, then why American? If the end has come, why not accept the discipline of the eschaton? If the end has not come, how to justify the revision of the Judaic consciousness and its reformation along Zionist lines? Nor has U.S. Jewry taken seriously the demands of logic and intellect for the formation of a credible ideology to explain the status quo and justify it.

"Enlandisement"

But the problem is not American alone, nor does it face only those who articulately espouse the Zionist idea. And, rightly understood, the problem is not a new one. The tension between ethnicism and religion, between "enlandisement" and universality, between Jewish nationalism and the mission of Israel, characterizes the history of the Jewish people and of Judaism throughout. Take, for example, the conflict of symbolism represented by Torah and Messiah. One achieves salvation through study of Torah and carrying out its precepts. *Or* one will be saved at the end of days by the Messiah of the House of David. But if Messiah, what need of Torah? And if Torah, why the Messiah? To be sure, the two are harmonized: If all Israel will keep a single Sabbath as the Torah teaches, then the Messiah will come. So the one is made to depend on the other. For the Talmudic rabbis, the Messiah depends upon Torah, and is therefore subordinate. Torah is an essentially particularist means of attaining salvation. Its observance is the obligation of Jews. Of all the commandments therein, only seven apply to non-Jews. The Messiah is primarily a universal figure. His action affects all mankind. Both nature and the nations, as much as Israel and its land, are the objects of his solicitude. Israel first, to be sure, but everyone at last comes to the end of days.

The tension between *holy land* and *holy Torah* as salvific symbols is pointed out by Abd al-Tafāhum in a remarkable essay, "Doctrine." [5] What is remarkable is that al-Tafāhum writes informedly and sympathetically about all three Middle Eastern religions. He says (p. 367), "The whole self-understanding of the Hebrews turns on 'enlandisement' and habitation and then, centuries later, on 'disenlandisement' and dispersion. Its two poles are Exodus and Exile . . . The triangular relationship is that of God, people, and territory."

With the Exile, the physical symbol is reenforced, and, in time, moved into the framework of the last things. Internalizing the effects of historical weakness, the Jews understood the exile as punishment for their sins in the land—"unrighteous tenancy"—and, as al-Tafāhum says, "The single theme of 'enlandisement' as the sign and pledge of the divine will and the human response" becomes paramount. To this is added a second understanding of Exile: "the nationhood to educate nations, the awareness of election and particularity that embraces a universal parable for all the segments of mankind and all the diversified economic and spiritual tenancies of terrestrial habitation by peoples and races in those interactions that make culture and history."

The meaning of Jewish history therefore becomes the philosophy of "experienced Zion"—an experience available both in the land and outside of it. The symbolism of Judaic religious experience was ever more shaped by having *and* not having the land. Having the land means standing in a proper relationship with the natural order. al-Tafāhum refers to A. D. Gordon: "everything creaturely

[5] Abd al-Tafāhum, "Doctrine," n A. J. Arberry, ed., *Religion in the Middle East* (Cambridge: Cambridge University Press, 1969), Vol. II, Part 2: THE THREE RELIGIONS IN CONCORD AND CONFLICT, pp. 365–412.

is material for sanctification . . . The land of promise is properly
not merely a divine bestowal but human fulfilment." Love of Zion
produces the marriage of Messiahship and kingship, land and
nation. Above all, it bears the intense particularities of Jewish
existence, the overwhelming love for Israel—land, people, faith—
characteristics of Jews through time.

"Disenlandisement," by contrast, produces the universal concern
of Israel for all people: the willingness to enter into intimate relationship with each and every civilization. Election stands over against
universality, but not wholly so: "Only you have I known among the
families of man, therefore I shall visit on you all your iniquities."
The unresolved tension in the history of Judaism is between privilege and particularity, on the one side, and the privilege of service
to men on the other. Unlike Christianity, Judaism never chose to
transcend its history, its intimacy with the Jews.

al-Tafāhum poses the question: "If Jewry disapproves the universalizing of its human mission which has happened in the Church,
how does it continue to reconcile its sense of privilege with the
self-transcending obligation, confessed and prized, within that very
identity?" Is Israel, the Jewish people, a mere ethnic continuity?
Can it equate spiritual vocation with biological persistence? "Can
the 'seed of Abraham' in any case be, in these times, a physically
guaranteed notion? Is destiny identical with heredity and fidelity
with birth? "Can [Jewry] either delegate its universal duty or realize
it merely by the percentage of literal seed?"

In former times, these questions found a response in the allega-
tion that Israel had a mission to carry out among the nations. Israel
was a presence within the world, "absorbing its values, using its
languages and participating in its life, while casting off, sometimes
almost in embarrassment, the distinctiveness of its own history and
cultic life." But that response has its limitations, for in discounting
the "historic elements of dogma and sanctity," Jews lost also all
sense of particularity and readily gave up what was unique to themselves to join the commonalities of mankind. The mission ended in
assimilation among those to be missionized.

Zionism, al-Tafāhum observes, "posits in new and more incisive
form the old question of universality." It contains within itself "an
ever sharper ambiguity about the final questions of the universal
meaning and obligation of the chosen people . . . By its own
deepest convictions Judaism is committed to the benediction of all
people and without this loyalty its very particularity is disqualified."

The question therefore stands: "Has the new 'enlandisement' betrayed the old? Was Diaspora the true symbol or the tragic negation
of what vocation meant? Are chosen-ness and the law, identity as
God's and duty to man, still proper and feasible clues to Jewish
existence? Or is the land now no more than the territorial location
of a secular nationality apostate from itself?" al-Tafāhum rightly

asserts that these issues are not of merely political interest, for "they reach most deeply into . . . the doctrinal heart." It would be difficult to improve upon this statement of the dilemma raised for modern Judaism by Zionism. If Zionism solves "the Jewish problem," it also creates interesting problems for Judaism.

A Hostile View

Zionism solves "the Jewish problem." Its success lies only partially in politics. The more profound problems for which it serves as a satisfactory solution are inward, spiritual, and, ultimately, religious. Just as the Judaic tradition had formerly told Jews what it meant to be Jewish—had supplied them with a considerable definition of their identity—so does Zionism in the modern age. Jews who had lost hold of the mythic structure of the past were given a grasp on a new myth, one composed of the restructured remnants of the old one.

The Jew had formerly been a member of a religious nation, believing in Torah revealed at Sinai, in one God who had chosen Israel, hoping for the Messiah and return to the land in the end of days. Jews who gave up that story of where they came from and who they are tell a new story based on the old, but in superficially secular form. To be Jewish means to live in the land and share in the life of the Jewish nation, which became the State of Israel.

To a hostile observer, things looked like this: The elements of "Jewishness" and the components of "Israelism" are to be one and the same—sacrifice, regeneration, resurrection. The sacrifice is no longer in the Temple; no prophets need decry the multitudes of fatted beasts. What now must be sacrificed is the blood of Israelis and the treasure of the Diaspora. The regeneration is no longer to be the turning of sinners to repentence—*teshuvah*—but rather the reformation of the economic and cultural realities of the Jewish people. No longer "parasites," but farmers, no longer dependent upon the cultural achievements of the nations but creators of a Hebrew, and "enlandised" culture, the Jews would be reborn into a new being and a new age. The resurrection is no longer of the dead at the end of time, but of the people at the end of the Holocaust.

The unfriendly witness sees matters this way: The new Zionist identity, like the old Judaic one, supplied a law for the rituals and attitudes of the faith. The old *halakhah* [law, way] was made irrelevant, the object of party-politics. The new was not partisan at all. All believed in, all fulfilled the law, except for sinners and heretics beyond the pale. The new law requires of Jewish man one great commandment: support Israel. Those who do it best, live there. Those who do not, pay a costly atonement in guilt and ransom for the absent body. The ransom is paid through the perpetual mobilization of the community in an unending campaign for funds. The guilt is exorcised through political rituals: letters to Congressmen and—for bourgeois Jews, what would normally be unheard of—mass rallies and street demonstrations. The guilt of Auschwitz and the sin of living in the Diaspora become intertwined: "On account of our sin do we live today, and in the wrong place at that!" Above all, the guilty and the sinner forever atone by turning to the *qiblah* [sacred place] of the land: There is no land but Israel, and the Jewish people are its product. The development of an American Jewish, or Judaic, culture is seen as irrelevant to the faith. The philanthropists will not support it, for no funds are left after allocations for Israel and for domestic humanitarian institutions. The rabbis will not speak of it, for the people will not listen. The people will hear of nothing but victories, and victories are won in this world, upon a fleshly battlefield, with weapons of war.

The old self-hatred . . . is left behind. No longer weak, one hardly needs to compensate for weakness by pretensions to moral superiority, and then to pay the price of that compensation by hatred of one's own weakness. Jews no longer look down on *goyim,* for they feel like them. The universal humanism, the cosmopolitanism of the old Jew are abandoned in the new particularism. The . . . grandmother who looked for Jewish names in reports of plane crashes has given way to the . . . grandson who turns off the news after the Middle Eastern reports are done with.

The Jew no longer makes contradictory demands on society. He no longer wants to be accepted into the tradition of society. In the new ethnicism of the hour, he seeks only his share. The liberal dilemma has been resolved. Jews now quite honestly interpret the universe in terms of their particular concerns. Self-hatred, liberalism, the crisis of identity—all fade into the background. The end of the old myths no longer matters much, for new ones have arisen in their place. The American Jews who did not want to be so Jewish that they could not also be part of the undifferentiated majority have had their wish fulfilled. Some have indeed ceased to be Jewish at all, and no one cares. Many others have found a place in the new, well-differentiated majority—so goes the hostile view.

The Zionist Problem

In what way, then, does Zionism constitute a problem for Judaism? In my view, it is not its secularity and worldliness, but the mythic insufficiency of Zionism that renders its success a dilemma for contemporary American Jews, and for Israeli ones as well.

Let us begin with the obvious. How can American Jews focus their spiritual lives *solely* on a land in which they do not live? It is one thing for that land to be in heaven, at the end of time, or across the Sambatyon for that matter. It is quite another to dream of a far-away place where everything is good—*but* where one may go if he wants. The realized eschaton is insufficient for a rich and interesting fantasy life, and, moreover, in this-worldly terms it is hypocritical. It means American Jews live off the capital of Israeli culture. Reliance on the State of Israel furthermore suggests that to satisfy their need for fantasy, American Jews must look forward to ever more romantic adventures reported in the press, rather than to the colorless times of peace. American Jews want to take their vacations among heroes, and then come home to the ordinary workaday world they enjoy and to which Israelis rightly aspire but do not own. The "enlandisement" of American Judaism—the focusing of its imaginative, inner life upon the land and State of Israel—therefore imposes an *ersatz* spiritual dimension. We live here *as if* we lived there—but do not choose to migrate.

It furthermore diverts American Judaism from the concrete mythic issues it has yet to solve: Why should anyone be a *Jew* anywhere, in the U.S.A. or in Israel? That question is not answered by the recommendation to participate in the spiritual adventures of people in a quite different situation. Since the primary *mitzvot* [commandments] of U.S. Judaism concern supplying funds, encouragement, and support for Israel, one wonders whether one must be a Jew at all in order to believe in and practice that form of Judaism. What is "being Jewish" now supposed to mean?

The underlying problem, which faces both Israeli and American Jews, is understanding what the ambiguous adjective *Jewish* is supposed to mean when the noun *Judaism* has been abandoned. To be sure, for some Israelis and American Jews to be a Jew is to be a citizen of the State of Israel—but that definition hardly serves when Israeli Moslems and Christians are taken into account. If one ignores the exceptions, the rule is still wanting. If to be a Jew is to be—or to dream of being—an Israeli, then the Israeli who chooses to settle in a foreign country ceases to be a Jew when he gives up Israeli citizenship for some other. If all Jews are on the road to Zion, then those who either do not get there or, once there, choose another way are to be abandoned. That makes Jewishness depend upon quite worldly issues: This one cannot make his living in Tel Aviv, that one does not like the climate of Affula, the other is frustrated by the bureaucracy of Jerusalem. Are they then supposed to give up their share in the "God of Israel"?

More seriously still, the complete "enlandisement" of Judaism for the first time since 586 B.C. forces the Judaic tradition to depend upon the historical fortunes of a single population in a small country. The chances for the survival of the Jewish people have surely been enhanced by the dispersion of the Jews among differing political systems. Until World War II Jews had stood on both sides of every international contest for most remote antiquity. Now, we enter an age in which the fate of Jewry and destiny of Judaism are supposed to depend on the fortunes of one state and one community alone.

That, to be sure, is not a fact, for even now the great Jewish communities in the U.S.S.R., Western Europe, Latin America, and North America, as well as smaller ones elsewhere, continue to conform to the historical pattern. But, ideologically, things have vastly changed. With all the Jewish eggs in one basket, the consequence of military actions is supposed to determine the future of the whole of Jewry and Judaism. So the excellence of some eight hundred pilots and the availability of a few dozen fighter-bombers are what it all comes down to. Instead of the thirty-six righteous men of classical myth are seventy-two phantoms—mirages—a curious revision of the old symbolism.

A Judaic Answer

Just what is *important* about being Jewish and in Judaism? In my view, the answer must pertain both to the State of Israel and to the *Golah* [diaspora] communities in equal measure. It cannot be right only for American Jewry, for we are not seeking a *Galut*-ideology, and no one would accept it. Such an ideology—right for here but irrelevant to Israelis—would obviously serve the selfish interests and the peculiar situation of American Jews alone. But the answer cannot pertain only to the situation of the Israeli Jews, for precisely the same reason.

What is important about being Jewish is the capacity of the Jewish people and its mythic creations to preserve the tension between the intense particularities of their life and the humanity they have in common with the rest of mankind. That tension, practically unique to Jewry, derives from its exceptional historical experience. Until now, it has been the basis for the Jews' remarkable role in human history.

Others have not felt such a tension. To be human and to be English—or Navaho—were hardly differentiated. And why should they have been, when pretty much everyone one cared for and knew was English, or Navaho? To be a Jew in any civilization was, and is, to share the values held by everyone *but* to stand in some ways apart (not above) from the others. It was, and is, to love one's native land with open arms, to preserve the awareness of other ways of living life and shaping culture.

To be sure, before the destruction of the First Temple in 586 B.C., Jewish people may well have been much like others. But from that time forward the land was loved with an uncommon intensity, for it had been lost, then regained, therefore could never again be taken for granted. And alongside land, the people found as few have *had* to, that Jews live by truths that could endure outside a single land and culture. Jewry discovered in itself an international culture, to be created and recreated in every land and in every language. It found in its central moral and ethical convictions something of value for all civilizations. Its apprehension of God and its peculiar method of receiving and spelling out revelation in the commonplaces of everyday life were divorced from a single place, even the holiest place in the world, where they had begun.

But al-Tafāhum is wrong in supposing that the Jews' "disenlandisement" was the precondition for the recognition of what was of universal importance about themselves. On the contrary, it was in the land itself that the awareness of ethnic differentiation proved the *least* vivid. Outside of it the group turned inward, and rightly so, for it became most acutely sensitive to its differences from others. In this respect the gentile students of Judaism do not understand what it is to be a Jew. The Diaspora Jew addresses himself to the nations and in their own language, but in doing so he speaks as a *Jew.* It is the "enlandised" Jew who sees himself as no different from everyone within his range of vision, therefore as man among men, rather than Jew among gentiles. The willingness and necessity to enter into intimate relationship with each and every civilization therefore produced two sorts of encounters, the one, between the Jewish man in his land and other men who might come there, or whom he might know elsewhere, men who held in common the knowledge of what it means to belong to some one place; the other, between the world and the always self-aware Jew, living in other lands, a Jew sensitive to the language and experience of those lands precisely because he was forever at the margins of the common life.

Jewry did not disapprove the universalizing of its mission in the Church. It simply did not recognize that the Church ever truly carried out that mission. Jewry perceived no discontinuity requiring reconciliation between its sense of peoplehood (privilege) and its "self-transcending obligation." The Jews long ago ceased to be a mere ethnic continuity, and no one, in either the State of Israel or the Diaspora, regards the Jews as merely an ethnic group. One can, after all, become a Jew by other than ethnic and territorial assimilation, through *conversion.* That fact predominates in all discussions of what it is to be a Jew. The issue comes from the other side: *Can* one become a Jew not through conversion, but through mere assimilation? The dogged resistance of Jewry to the reduction of Jewishness to ethnicity alone testifies to the falseness of al-Tafāhum's reading of the Jewish situation.

But his other question is indeed troubling: Is destiny to be equated with heredity and fidelity with birth? The answer to that question can be found only in the working out of the potentialities of both Israeli and Diaspora Jewish life.

To be sure, the old Diaspora—the one before 1948—absorbed the values of the nations and could locate no one center where the distinctiveness, hence the universality, of Jewish history and civilization might be explored. Zionism does indeed posit in new and more incisive form the old question of universality, *but it also answers that question*. In the Jewish state Jews lose their sense of peculiarity. They reenter the human situation common to everyone but Jews. In the State of Israel everyone is Jewish, therefore no one is the Jew. And this, in my view, opens the way to an interesting development: the reconsideration of Jewish humanity in relationship with the other sorts of humanity in the world. It is now possible for the normal to communicate with the normal.

What the Israelis have to communicate is clear to one and all. They have not divorced themselves from important elements of the Jewish past, but have retained and enhanced them. The possession of the land, after all, represents such an important element. What does it mean to believe that one's moral life is somehow related to the destiny of the land in which one lives? In times past the question would have seemed nonsensical. But today no people is able to take its land, its environment, for granted. Everyone is required to pay attention to what one does with one's blessings. Today each land is endangered by immoral men who live upon and make use of it. The moral pollution of which the prophets spoke may infect not only a society but the way a society makes use of its resources. So the intimate relationship between Israel and the land is no longer so alien to the existence of other nations. And the ecological-moral answers found in the land and State of Israel are bound to have universal meaning.

I choose this example because it is the least obvious. The record of the State of Israel is, in my view, not ambiguous about "the final questions of the universal meaning and obligation of the chosen people." One need not be an Israeli apologist to recognize the numerous ways in which the State of Israel has sought to make war without fanaticism, to wage peace with selflessness. Only indifference to the actual day to day record of the State of Israel, with its technical assistance, its thirst for peace, its fundamentally decent society at home, and above all its hatred of what it must do to survive, justifies questions concerning Israel's "universal duty." On the contrary, it seems to me that Israeli society has, within the limits of its wisdom and power, committed itself to the benediction of all peoples, and with its loyalty to that very blessing its very particularity is verified and justified.

I therefore do not agree that the new "enlandisement" has betrayed the old. It has fulfilled it.

The other half of the question pertains to the Diaspora. The Diaspora was neither the true symbol nor the tragic negation of Israel's vocation. "Chosenness and law, obligation to God and duty to man," are still proper and feasible clues to Jewish existence both at home and abroad. The land never was, and is not now, merely the territorial locus of a secular nationality. The existence of the Diaspora guarantees otherwise. The Diaspora supplies the certainty that men of many languages and civilizations will look to Zion for more than a parochial message, just as the Israelis make certain the Diaspora Jews will hear that message. But, as I said, things are the reverse of what al-Tafāhum supposes. The Diaspora brings its acute *consciousness of being different* from other men, therefore turns to the State to discover the ways in which it is like the others. The Diaspora contributes its variety and range of human experience to the consciousness of the State of Israel. But the State offers the Diaspora the datum of normality.

One cannot divide the Jewish people into two parts, the "en-landised" and the "disenlandised." Those in the land look outward. Those outside look toward the land. Those in the land identify with the normal peoples. Those abroad see in the land what it means to be extraordinary. But it is what happens to the whole, altogether, that is decisive for the Judaic tradition. And together, the Diaspora Jew and the Israeli represent a single tradition, a single memory. That memory is of having had a land and lost it—*and* never having repudiated either the memory of the land *or* the experience of living elsewhere. No one in the State of Israel can imagine that to be in the land is for the Jew what being in England is to the Englishman. The Englishman has never lost England and come back. So one cannot distinguish between the Israeli and the Diaspora Jew. Neither one remembers or looks upon a world in which his particular values and ideals are verified by society. Neither ceases to be cosmopolitan. Both preserve a universal concern for *all* Israel. Both know diversities of culture and recognize therefore the relativity of values, even as they affirm their own.

This forms what is unique in the Jewish experience: the denial of men's need to judge all values by their particular, self-authenticating system of thought. In this regard the Diaspora re-enforces the Israeli's view of the world, and the Israeli reciprocates. Both see as transitory and merely useful what others understand to be absolute and perfected. Behind the superficial eschatological self-confidence of Zionism lies an awareness everywhere present that that is just what Zionism adds up to: a *merely* secular eschatology. No one imagines that Zionism has completed its task or that the world has been perfected. The world is seen by both parts of the Jewish people to be insufficient and incomplete.

The Israelis' very sense of necessity preserves the Jews' neatest insight: without choice, necessity imposes duty, responsibility, un-imagined possibilities. The Jews are not so foolish as to have for-gotten the ancient eternal cities—theirs and others'—which are no more. They know therefore that it is not the place, but the quality of life within it, that truly matters. No city is holy, not even Jerusa-lem, but men must live in some one place and assume the responsibilities of the mundane city. But if no city is holy, at least Jerusalem may be made into a paradigm of sanctity. Though all they have for mortar may be slime, Jewish men will indeed build what they must, endure as they have to. The opposite is not to wander, but to die.

But have Diaspora Jews strayed so far from those same truths? In sharing the lives of many civilizations, do they do other than to assume responsibility for place? Do they see the particular city as holy, because they want to sanctify life in it? Or do they, too, know that the quality of life *anywhere* is what must truly matter? Men must live in some one place, and so far as Jewish men have something to teach of all they have learned in thirty centuries, they should live and learn and teach in whatever place they love. And one may err if he underestimates the capacity of the outsider, of the Diaspora Jew, to love.

I therefore see no need either to repudiate Zionism or to give up the other elements that have made *being Jewish* a magnificent mode of humanity. Zionism, on the contrary, supplies Jewry with still another set of experiences, another set of insights into what it means to be human. Only those who repudiate the unity of Israel, the Jewish people, in favor of either of its segments can see things otherwise. But viscerally American Jews know better, and I think they are right in refusing to resolve the tensions of their several commitments. Zionism creates problems for Judaism only when Zionists think that all that being Jewish means is "enlandisement" and, thereby, redemption. But Zionists *cannot* think so when they contemplate the range of human needs and experiences they as men must face. Zionism is a part of Judaism. It cannot be made the whole, because Jews are more than people who need either a place to live or a place on which to focus fantasies. The profound existential necessities of Jews—both those they share with every man and those they have to themselves—are not met by Zionism or "enlandisement" alone. Zionism provides much of the vigor and excitement of contemporary Jewish affairs, but so far as Jews live and suffer, are born and die, reflect and doubt, raise children and worry over them, love and work—so far as Jews are human, they require Judaism.[6]

Having participated as a protagonist in the analysis of Zionism, the writer can scarcely reclaim the role of interpreter and onlooker, bilingual guide for the interested visitor. It does seem, however, that the ambiguities of Zionism—its curious amalgamization of the most modern and secular with the most archaic and religious—do testify accurately to the ambiguities of American Judaism, and, beyond them, to the equivocal modernity of modern man.

[6] Jacob Neusner, "Judaism and the Zionist Problem," *Judaism*, XIX, No. 3 (Summer, 1970), 311–14, 315–16, 317–23.

Why do modern men find it necessary to retain messianic fervor when they have long since abandoned belief in a Messiah? How do thoroughly secular people reconcile the desacralization of place with the fervent belief in the centrality of a quite undistinguished strip of Mediterranean litoral? Perhaps all we have before us is mere sentimentality, the meretricious appropriation of memories of things that no one believes really happened or, if they did, no longer actually matter.

On the other hand, the puzzling, unexpected conversion to Zionism of the larger part of American Jewry may tell us something about the insufficiency of modernity for the human condition, the need to create new myths out of the ruins of old ones, the abiding quest for felt-meaning in routine history, and the persistent search for something to do beyond mere workaday living. We may well witness something more than a political and sociological fact, a response to political and sociological conditions. The Jews' assertion that beliefs are facts, not matters of faith, is peculiarly modern, for modern men do not believe things, they merely *know* them to be true. But the substance of the Zionist "faith," all the more so its integrative capacity and generative force— these testify to unanticipated continuities with the archaic and traditional world of classical Judaism. At the root of the life of archaic, as of modern, men is the quest for meaning for the lives of individuals and of groups. Without the capacity to supply that meaning for Jews, Zionism would be merely what it claimed, a quite secular, political movement. But without that capacity, Zionism could not have succeeded, as it has, in winning the support of the masses of Jews and shaping their view of themselves as men.

chapter 5

HOLY TORAH

UNTIL NOW WE HAVE FOCUSED OUR ATTENTION on issues central to modern Judaism but not characteristic of religions in modern America. Our concern has been for the sides of modern Judaic expression that are peculiar to the religiosity of Jews: their expression of their group life primarily through secular organizations; their exceptional revision of the role of religious leaders; their crisis of identity and consequent self-hatred; and their concentration upon the "redemption" to be attained through a political movement. Other American religions would have included in the "holy way" some attention to sacraments and other religious deeds; in the "holy man," a measure of consideration of the intrinsic sanctity of ordination and the liturgical role of the minister or priest; in the "holy people," concern for the life of the church-community; and in the "holy land," an awareness of last things, heaven, life after death, and related other-worldly matters. It now is time to address ourselves to issues faced in common by Judaism and the other American religious traditions, issues of the life of the church—here, the synagogue, study of Torah, and theology.

Since "Torah" in classical Judaism both symbolized and comprehended what "religion" does in the study of religions, our examination of contemporary American Judaism can best start with an account of synagogue life of American Jews from Arthur Hertzberg's "The American Jew and His Religion."

The evidence continues to mount in support of the fact that about three-fifths of all the Jews in America today, in 1964, are affiliated with a synagogue. In close to two decades since the end of World War II, we have witnessed the greatest single synagogue-building boom in the whole of Jewish history in the Diaspora. This has taken place in the very same years during which the American Jewish community has been giving hundreds of millions of dollars towards strengthening the new state of Israel. The attendance of the Jewish young upon some form of Jewish education at some time during their early years has now reached the figure of over eighty percent. It is unusual for a thirteen-year-old nowadays not to be Bar Mitzvah.

Atheism is no longer a recognizable force in the American Jewish community, though it was quite prevalent in the immigrant radical movements fifty years ago. The central institutions of the major religious denominations have flourished in recent years as never before. Among the Orthodox, the Yeshiva University has been transformed from the small struggling school of the 1930's to a major center of Jewish and secular learning. The Jewish Theological Seminary, the central institution of Conservative Judaism, and its allied bodies have at least tripled in size in the last generation. More recently, the influence of Conservative Judaism has been spreading to countries overseas and even to Israel. Reform Judaism has benefited comparably: in the growing strength of its synagogue body, the Union of American Hebrew Congregations; in increases in staff and facilities at its rabbinical seminary, which now has major centers both in Cincinnati and New York; and in its spread, too, to other countries.

This brief sketch of the current scene evokes the image of a religious community which is mindful of and responsible to its Jewish heritage and clearly committed to continuing Judaism in its various contemporary forms. There is, however, a negative side to the picture. Jews do belong to synagogues at least to the degree to which Protestants and Catholics by birth identify with their churches, but it is notorious that, except for the High Holidays, synagogue attendance is radically lower than church attendance. Various studies that have been made in recent years all point to the same conclusion: half of the enrolled Christians, with variations among the persuasions, go to church regularly on Sunday; no more than one, or at most two, in ten of Jews who belong to a synagogue, are there regularly at the Sabbath services.

Nowadays almost all of the Jewish young are attending college. What we are discovering about the religious views and observances of this generation is therefore of great importance. Various studies agree that almost all Catholic college students and most Protestants believe in God; a substantial number among the Jewish students classify themselves as atheists. Attendance at High Holiday worship on campus, in the years when college begins too early for the students to be at home with their parents, is known to be quite spotty. A growing number, perhaps a third, of the students at the most intellectual schools have been declaring themselves as not at all opposed to intermarriage; these views are indeed reflected in a rate of marrying out that now approaches fifteen percent.

The estate of Jewish observance in the American Jewish community must be added to the negative phenomena. To be sure, everyone observes Hanukkah, but the same "everyone" knows that this is a form of dealing with the problem of Christmas. Obedience to the dietary laws, which are mandatory among both the Orthodox and the Conservative, has declined disastrously. A study of the most committed element of the Conservative laity, the members of the boards of congregations, has demonstrated that even in such circles no more than one in three keep completely *kosher* homes. American Orthodoxy is substantially more obedient in this area, but even among this element one-third does not observe *kashrut*. Notoriously, only a small minority of American Jews, mostly to be found among the Orthodox, observe the Sabbath in their personal behavior.

Thus, there is the image of growing numbers, economic prosperity of the religious institutions, and increasing power of the denominational central bodies. Indeed, in relative terms this generation has witnessed the shift of influence within the American Jewish community from the secular organizations which dominated the scene in the 1930's to the religious bodies which, on every level, are increasingly holding the foreground in the 1960's. On the other hand, religion is ultimately not institutions and structures, or even success in adapting to a changing scene. It is faith, and the personal conduct which flows from it. In that deepest dimension Jewish religion in America is failing amidst its great pragmatic successes.

In organizational terms, each of the three major groups within American Judaism today possesses well-developed, comparable structures. The earliest to be created were . . . those of Reform Judaism. It is probable that there are today about a million Jews affiliated with Reform congregations. There are 650 congregations identified with the Union of American Hebrew Congregations. More than 850 rabbis belong to the Central Conference of American Rabbis. From social action to education there is well-developed programming at the two national headquarters of Reform [Judaism] in New York and Cincinnati. The Conservatives started later in the creation of their institutions. Their synagogue body was not organized until 1913, but the United Synagogue of America today numbers almost 800 congregations within its ranks. The enrolled strength of the Conservative movement is well over one million; moreover, because this is the middle-of-the-road group, the unaffiliated tend to look to it rather than to the other two as their own. All the recent studies of religious preference, as seperate from formal affiliation, show almost unvaryingly that about half the Jews in America regard themselves as Conservative. The Rabbinical Assembly of America, the organization of Conservative rabbis, has a membership approaching 800. The Union of Orthodox Jewish Congregations claims all those synagogues which are not formally identified with the other two groups, some 2,500. Certainly nowhere near that number pay dues to that body. In all its varieties, from English-speaking liberal Orthodoxy to the most recent Yiddish-speaking Hasidic enclaves, Orthodoxy in America today commands the allegiance of perhaps one million Jews. In the Orthodox rabbinate, the Rabbinical Council of America numbers 800; the Agudath ha-Rabbanim perhaps 600; and there are many who are not affiliated with either body. To this day, despite some notable successes of the other two groups in producing their own religious leaders, the Orthodox remain the major suppliers of rabbis for all the divisions of American Jewry, since this group produces all of its own clergy and at least a substantial minority of those who serve the other two groups.

The leadership of the major denominations, and of the various schools within them, have labored for decades to define theological differences among them. This has been particularly marked on the theological left, in the efforts of the Reconstructionists, and in the continuing ferment among the Orthodox, especially as they have battled against the inroads within their group of such Conservative practices as mixed seating. In theory, all the Orthodox groups agree on the revealed nature of all the Jewish law; for the Reform group the moral doctrine of Judaism is divine and its ritual law is man-made; the Conservatives see Judaism as the working out in both areas of a divine revelation that is incarnate in a slowly changing and adjusting human history; the Reconstructionists view Judaism as the evolving civilization created by the Jewish people in the light of its highest conscience. But assent cannot be produced in each group for even these minimal definitions. What really marks the various bodies in the mind of the Jewish community is their differences in ritual practice. The Reform, in their overwhelming majority, disregard dietary laws; the Orthodox are committed formally to obey every jot and tittle of them. Even the leaders of Conservative Judaism are, in practice, usually sufficiently liberal about *kashrut* to permit themselves to dine out on food that is not in and of itself *trefah* [not *kosher*] regardless of the dishes on which it is prepared. All but the Reform wear hats at divine service, and that custom is slowly returning to some Reform congregations. Only the Orthodox separate the sexes in the synagogue, but the practice is bit by bit becoming less prevalent in English-speaking Orthodox congregations. We are, in reality, on the religious scene confronted by a continuum, at least in native-born circles, in which the ritual variations shade from one group into the other. Each of the groups still has a distinctive character, based on the nature of the majority of its congregations, but the dissimilarities have clearly lessened. Predictions are dangerous but it is not unlikely that in fifty years the three denominational groups will continue to exist; this will, however, represent more the momentum of their separate organizational strengths than any sharpening of theological and ritual differences.

That American Jewish religion is in many senses a continuum is evident, in part, in the freedom with which many people change denominational allegiance as they move. Their choice is very often the nearest synagogue rather than the one that is denominationally the same as the synagogue they just left. This phenomenon is more evident still in the role of the rabbi in the American Jewish religious community. It is substantially the same in all three groups. Not even among the Orthodox, except for a few renowned authorities in the field of talmudic law, is the rabbi today much occupied with rendering decisions on Jewish practice. He is everywhere a preacher, chief executive officer of a congregation, pastor, and moving spirit in the synagogue's educational program. With some variations of emphasis, denominations expect their rabbis to be communal leaders in Jewish affairs and representative figures in the general community. Jewish scholarship, in either its classic or modern forms, is rather low on the list of what congregations demand from their clergy. There are, indeed, a few notable scholars in the practicing rabbinate in America today, but their learning is more a matter of personal predilection than of communal demand. In short, the rabbi in America today is a cross between a pastor or parish priest and the leader of an ethnic group. The East European . . . tradition produced, at its very end, two images of a proper spiritual leader: either that of the Lithuanian tradition—profound learning—or that of the Hasidic tradition—holiness. The American rabbi today is rich in eloquence, organizational talent, and practical achievement; the American scene has evoked neither intellectual endeavor nor transcendent piety, but it has not done so in American Christianity either. The most Jewish figure on the American scene, the rabbi, is thus in many senses the most American.[1]

Two further aspects of Torah require attention. First, since study of Torah was a predominately religious ideal, on the one hand, and intellectual effort was the worldly expression of that ideal, on the other, we must ask: What has become of the intellectual enterprise of classical Judaism? Arthur A. Cohen supplies a picture of the two traditions of Jewish intellectuality, archaic and modern.

[1] Arthur Hertzberg, "The American Jew and His Religion," in Oscar I. Janowsky, ed., *The American Jew: A Reappraisal* (Philadelphia: Jewish Publication Society, 1964), pp. 101–103, 115–17.

There are two traditions of the Jewish intellectual: one is ancient, the other modern; one enjoyed illustrious pretension and achievement and, only in our day, has come on ill-fortune; the other began in dialectical tension and counterpoint to classic Judaism and, only in our day, has defined itself in alienation from classic Judaism; the one was religious, indeed philosophic, in posture; the other is not only secular, but hostile to religion and, what is more surprising, indifferent, if not bored, by speculative philosophy. The "ghetto" of the religious despises the "ghetto" of the secular as theologically illiterate and unJewish; the conventicle of the secular regards that of the religious to be parochial, conservative, and un-modern. The fact that the religious are energized and, in a measure, unified by their single-minded hostility to and incomprehension of the secular Jewish intellectual is not recognized. The fact that the secular Jewish intellectual derives much of his self-definition as Jew and intellectual from his spirited and deliciously painful alienation from the community of traditional Jews is equally ignored. Without the palpable pressures of the other, both ghettoes would be obliged to function with different criteria of cohesion and membership; both would be compelled to ask different questions of themselves; both, in effect, would be constrained to end their ghettodom. It is surely ironic that the gentile Christian world which was responsible for the original ghetto is no longer responsible for the persistence of the Jewish ghettoes of the present day. The Jews, however—both the traditional and the secular—*are* responsible. They need each other and the radiant warmth and reassurance of their own circle and their own malaise to guarantee their existence. They need to pinch (and occasionally mutilate) the flesh of their own to know that they are yet alive.

The Jewish intellectual is a modern phenomenon. Neither the Sage nor the Scholar needed to be intellectuals, and it is the Scholar and Sage, the Righteous Man and the Prophet, who are the models of Jewish tradition. They are paradigmatic persons, for they contain all the perfections of a sacred tradition. They are normative, rather than rare and exceptional occurrences, for it is to them that the Jew should turn, when defining for himself the task of his own life. Moreover, they exist and have existed; they can be named and their lives narrated; they have influenced and continue to influence. But they are still models, for there are no rules or guides by which to be instructed in achieving what they achieved nor are there manuals and directions for their imitation. They are finally beyond time and history, caught up in mythology, legend, hagiography. It is known when such exemplary sages and saints—Rabbi Akiba, and Rabbi Hillel, Maimonides and Yehuda Halevi, Rabbi Elijah Goan of Vilna and Rabbi Israel Baal Shem Tov—lived and died, with whom they were conversant and by what influence they were formed, but the whole of their lives is still clouded by mystery—and not simply a mystery which additional information might some day dispel, but one which is essential to the awe and reverence with which they are regarded. They are paradigms to Jewish tradition, *a priori* models.

The model of the Jewish Sage and Saint, the classic source and progenitor of the contemporary traditionalist, was first defined by the Hebrew Bible and the Rabbinic literature. The Bible is regarded by traditional Jews as a record of the meeting, covenant, and portentous encounter of God and a People whom he chose out of all the peoples of the earth to bring near to him, to instruct and form, to raise up from historical insignificance and educate, that they might—in attendance upon his tutelage—become, in their own person, themselves a paradigm to all the nations of the earth, in turn instructing them, setting for them an example, bringing them near to the single and unique God, the Lord of time and history. God is the sublime object of imitation for the Jew, and in the Jewish imagination, all the virtues to which the Jew aspires are ascribed to God: God is seen by the rabbis as a studious and learned God, attending to the study of Scripture and its Commentaries, conducting in the after-life a vast Talmudic Academy to which all those deserving and undeserving in the House of Israel are assembled in study and contemplation; as a pious and observant God, donning his phylacteries and saying his prayers, attending to feasts and festivals, remembering to say Kaddish and pay his obsequies to the great among his favored dead; and a Lord of history, conspiring to raise up Israel from the dust, to renovate her conscience, to bring forth from her midst the Messiah, whose name he has known since immemorial times before even the world was created. If, then, such a God reveals the truth—showing forth in the person of his perfect imitators, his Sages, Saints, Heroes, Martyrs, the order of his perfection, displaying in the counsels of the Torah the laws and requirements of his realm—it is clear that those who would wish to be faithful to his covenant with them, should bend their years to the study of his work, to the understanding of his demands, to the fulfillment of his expectations.

The Jewish Sage could continue to define the model of excellence for Jewry only so long as the conditions of European culture were favorable—that is, favorably hostile and unyielding. The social institution of the ghetto, the *Juderia* and *aljama,* afforded the Jew an insulated environment, which, however open to the ravages of Prince and Bishop, was still set off and protected to a degree from the irrational terrorization of burgher and peasant. Jewish life in the ghetto, though no more halcyon than the life of dependents anywhere during the Middle Ages, was still privileged. Undoubtedly the first international people in European culture, Jews maintained mercantile and banking connections throughout Europe which were valuable and negotiable. Although *servi camerae,* as Frederick I first defined them, they were better off than Christian serfs—protected by the local Prince for his own financial reasons, granted rights of self-determination and local autonomy, succored and bid for. Within the ghetto, however, Jewish life was predominantly religious, a life girded by Torah, piety, worship, and study. In such a world the Sage and the *Zaddik* could hold dominion.

The Jew was an accidental beneficiary and victim of the rise of nationalism and the diffusion of the spirit of enlightenment throughout Western Europe in the eighteenth century: beneficiary in that the irrepressible logic of revolutionary egalitarianism could not help but include, and therefore, however reluctantly, liberate the Jew; and victim in that the price demanded for the Jew's free entry into European society was self-divestment of all those irrational legacies which rendered him separate, distinct, and autonomous within European society. Everything that the Jew had been in order to withstand Christendom and endure as a living rebuke to Christianity was now being asked by a less militant and unsacerdotal society as the price for admission to its world. The Jew was not unaware that what was being asked was that he cease to be a Jew. What the Christian was not aware was that *he* was not prepared, just yet, to complete his half of the bargain. The Christian was not ready to give up Christianity, although he had already begun to transform it from an urgency for which he was prepared to go to war against his neighbor into a social utility whose viciousness and snobbism increased almost in direct proportion to the degree to which he had ceased to believe in it.

The nineteenth century Jewish intellectuals who elaborated the "survivalist" ideologies of modern Judaism—*Wissenschaft des Judentums,* political and cultural Zionism, cultural autarchy, the Hebrew renaissance, the various forms of messianic Socialism—were, by and large, still working against the pressures and insistence of commanding traditional models. However one estimates the activity of Leopold Zunz and his circle, the extraordinary Moses Hess, or later, that of the poets, Bialik and Tchernichovsky, or Simon Dubnow and Ahad Ha-Am, or the German neo-Kantian philosopher Hermann Cohen, one is obliged to recognize that for these thinkers (regardless of how little they prayed, or how little observed, or how obliquely and disinterestedly they regarded theological questions) the center of their life was the Jewish People. The Jewish People was for them as it was for their millennial ancestors the primary chord of identity. The Jewish People was source and bearer, legator and legatee, conduit and destiny. For them the question was: of what? bearer, sustainer, viaticum of what? For some, of pain and suffering, to be assuaged by courage and hard work, by redefinition and consecration to political and revolutionary goals or to the building of a new land. For others, of the most profound moral and ethical truths which, quarried from superstition and ritualism, would renew all mankind.

These Jewish intellectuals could not conceive of their function as intellectuals independently of their existence as Jews. This is not to say that they did not try, that for many the bringing to union the power of their own conception with the unavoidable fact of their Jewishness was not an unceasing struggle. Rather, what is being suggested is that for them the nexus of intellect and the people had replaced the sundered bond of faith and people. The Jew could no longer regard the certitudes of faith as sufficient to accommodate itself to the Jewish requirement to stay alive as Jews. It is of course the case that Hermann Cohen was an astonishingly nationalistic German; and that Eastern European Jewish intellectuals often wrote masterfully in Russian and Polish as well as Yiddish and Hebrew. But for Hermann Cohen, son of a *Hazzan* from Coswig and Professor at the University of Marburg, the issue was finding the link which would inextricably unite Kant and Goethe with the Bible and the Rabbis; while for that autonomist Dubnow, for example, the Jewish community he dreamed of building in Lithuania, Poland, or Russia would be intimately conversant with the best thinking in non-Jewish intellectual and cultural life. For those Jewish intellectuals, there was a struggle against compartmentalization, a disinclination to build a dualism into their intellectual life, to separate out Blake, Donne and Wordsworth as "real literature" and leave the medieval Spanish and Provençal Jewish poets, or the Kabbalah and Hasidic mystics to a restricted self, tolerated and smiled upon, but regarded implicitly as inferior.

All this is now past. Such Jewish intellectuals for whom being Jewish was a destiny as well as a fate, have by and large disappeared, and they have not been replaced. This is not to say that there are no more Jewish intellectuals, but that those who exist are astonishingly different from their forebears. The new Jewish intellectual, although he still works against the classic sacral models of scholar, sage and prophet, has turned these models away from Judaism and into self-sustaining ideological postures. He depends for his passion and preoccupations upon the impossibility that society should have fulfillment beyond the work of human planning, intelligence, and imagination. The dream of the social reformer and radical intellectual of the thirties is now the blunted, too often cynical, craftsmanship of the sixties. One can speak here less dogmatically for one speaks of one's contemporaries and they can rarely be observed dispassionately or correctly. What one senses, however, is that the Jewish intellectual of a generation ago was still dealing with potencies and skills wrenched from the context of traditional Jewish life. He was still a messianist, although he no longer believed the Messiah would come as tradition conceived him. He still believed in the transformation and the apotheosis of history, although his historical intelligence had completed the debunking of any eschatological doctrine. He could still believe that the *yetzer hatov* [good impulse], once liberated and reinforced, could triumph over avarice, social distress, poverty, and war. Today such secular messianism would be regarded as naive and sentimental, and moreover a naivete and sentimentalism as unavoidably Jewish in origin as it was Saint Simonian and socialist. The innocence has gone out of the Jewish intellectual.

The new Jewish sage is totally immersed in history. He is the man who knows more about the Sino-Russian split than the Supreme Soviet, more about Chinese Marxism, more about Fidel Castro and Cuba, more about everything—even though, by and large, he is not professionally engaged in forming or effectuating government policy and disdains such occupation. The new Jewish intellectual is an expert in a society of experts. He is the man who knows how the institutions of society work, what can be expected of men and what has to be dragged out of them. He is still a Jew, but like a latter-day, sharpened version of the *maskil* [enlightened] in Yiddish fiction, he is more cynical and somehow less humane; he has employed his talents and powers not to bring an end to the historical ghetto of the traditional intellectuals, to open up to the whole of human culture the resource and energies of traditional Juadism—long sequestered and undisclosed—but rather has employed his gifts too readily to define the society of an "in-ghetto," "an establishment ghetto," a ghetto which is inhabited largely by Jews familiar with an intellectual shorthand, a socio-political jargon, an arcanum of concerns which seem often narrow, purblind, and unproductive.

There is no *tertium quid,* no third force between the Jewish scholar on the one hand and the new Jewish intellectual on the other. It is however the third force which is so desperately needed, not only that an entente be established, a kind of parlous truce, but rather that a communication be entered upon which will have the purpose of renewing the valid vocation of Torah for the scholar and enable the Jewish intellectual to make an educated decision for himself respecting Judaism. The third force is the unaligned believer, the Jew who is neither with the party of the institution nor with the *dernier cri* of the omniscient intellectual. Perhaps, what is needed is a recovery for the contemporary Jew of what Franz Rosenzweig had been for the German Jews of his generation; a third option, radically alone and individual and yet wholly immersed in the urgencies of history: open and present before the claims of both Christianity and revolutionary Marxism and yet temporizing both claimants by making the anti-political impotence of historical Judaism into a positive device of peace; compelling Judaism to make itself a witness to the non-Jewish world, to the un-Jewish world, to the world that doesn't even know that Judaism exists. What is needed is in effect to charge Judaism with the burden of an almost Erasmian revolution, a humanist counterpoint to both Christianity and Marxism, which avoids both traditional obscurantism and tedious litanies of Jewish self-hatred, which exposes not simply what is best in Judaism as a one-among-many good and suitable doctrines, but what is unqualifiedly best precisely because of its concern to afford the world a vision totally disconnected from the instrumentalities of power, whether sacerdotal or secular.

There can be an end to the Jewish ghetto, but the end of this ghettodom is the renaissance of Judaism. If it is truly the case that Judaism is hopelessly consecrated to ethnocentric, national, parochial concerns, whether political or religious, then our preoccupation with the existence or disappearance of the ghetto will be beside the point, for the vitalities of the "Jewish" in the Jew—which depend upon his willingness to entertain freedom and risk on behalf of historical destiny—will atrophy and disappear. The end of ghettodom is rather a recollection, a divine *anamnesis,* of the sacral model, the recall to history of the hero, Prophet and Sage who have stood for centuries beyond the borders of historical conflict, who served only as wraiths and tempters to the Jewish imagination, distant, ancient, remote, unavailing to the historical anguish into which the modern Jew has been obliged to descend.[2]

The "study of Torah" persists in the classical mode. America provides a healthy setting for the maintenance of Yeshivot, or classical schools for the study of Talmud and related sacred sciences, in the ancient manner. At the same time, "study of Torah" has produced a modern form, one in which the ancient themes of Judaic theology are developed in a modern idiom and made relevant to the situation of modern men. Lou H. Silberman provides an account of Judaic theology in the 1960's, and Eugene Borowitz offers comments on the coming age.

At the beginning of the decade 1958–1968, the chronological framework of this paper, the editor of *Judaism* offered as a note to the essay "The Question of Jewish Theology" by Jakob J. Petuchowski the comment, "The revival, in our day, of Jewish theology raises, if only by implication, at least two fundamental questions: Does Judaism need a theology? Is Jewish theology possible today?" The following examination of some of the writings and discussions during this period that concerned themselves with consideration of Judaism, its basic concepts, ideas, attitudes, beliefs, indeed suggests the questions may have been beside the point. For need or no need, possibility or no possibility, thinkers of a variety of persuasions, writers from a multitude of ambients, discussants from more than a few points of view, individual as well as institutional, have been busily engaged in doing theology.

2 Arthur A. Cohen, "Between Two Traditions," *Midstream,* XII, No. 6 (June/July, 1966), 26–27, 28–29, 31–33, 34.

Indeed, one is faced, quantitatively at least, with the proverbial *embarras de richesse*. During the decade there have appeared forty issues each of the *Central Conference of American Rabbis Journal, Conservative Judaism,* and *Tradition,* to point to professionally oriented "party" organs; the same was the number for *Judaism* (published by the secularist American Jewish Congress, but hardly a "party" organ). The American Jewish Committee's *Commentary,* directed to the intellectual and not primarily devoted to religious or necessarily Jewish interests, went to press one hundred and twenty times. The *Reconstructionist,* whose party label does not make it inhospitable to other points of view, appeared some two hundred times. In addition, the house organs of the ecclesiastical institutions and of the various secularist organizations must be counted in. The publications of various learned societies, non-Jewish as well as Jewish, also contain material falling within the range of this paper's interest. And then, of course, there are the books and monographs.

Thus, a survey in the magisterial form of some European journals, critically sifting all the books, articles, reviews, notes and communications comprising the total output, would easily exhaust both space limits and patience. The alternative to such a procedure (that it is being rejected casts no shadow upon its desirability and value) is the more vulnerable undertaking of discussing what this writer considers to have been the dominant themes, the crucial tensions, the significant developments of the decade's thought. In the circumstances, names mentioned are generally illustrative, although it ought to be assumed that the author's prejudices are unconsciously, if not consciously, at work. Further, it should be noted that not all or even the majority of the materials pointed to above were examined.

If the spring-flood of writings suggests that the editorial note to "The Question of Jewish Theology" about the need and possibility of Jewish theology is beside the point, Petuchowski's insistence that, in a predicted emergent situation, "the only possible form of Jewish existence in the Diaspora will be the *religious* existence" does indicate something of the problem at the root of the discussion during the decade.

More than a decade ago, Nathan Glazer, in his *American Judaism,* examined the relationship between Judaism and Jewishness and argued that the latter was then everywhere in retreat, while the former "showed a remarkable, if ambiguous, strength." According to C. Bezalel Sherman, whom Glazer cited, the reason may have been that secularism, i.e. *yidishkayt,* was being forced to wear the garb of the religious establishment in order to survive on the American scene, where cultural pluralism was dead. The import of this paradox of an ever more secular society defining allowable differences in terms of religious groupings was developed during that decade in its most ambitious form by Will Herberg in his volume

Protestant-Catholic-Jew. If diaspora existence was to be religious existence or, perhaps more accurately, existence as a religious (i.e., ecclesiastical) institution, it required, intellectually, a body of reflective thought interpreting the structures, forms, and institutions of that existence—theology. Thus viewed, theology serves the apologetic function of providing an intellectual structure for a community forced by its historical setting to appropriate a churchly mode of existence. There is no doubt that consciously or unconsciously such an apologetic motivation helped determine the development during the decade, and therefore must be taken into account. But to make it the sole or predominant factor is to misjudge the situation. Thus a new perspective is needed.

The immediate postwar years saw a tremendous upsurge in theological discussion among American Protestants. The full impact of what unfortunately has been called neo-orthodox thought (neo-Reformation would be a more satisfactory term), closely associated with Reinhold Neibuhr of the Union Theological Seminary in New York, began to make itself fully felt. The promises of liberal theology that had been part of the optimism still pervading the American scene in the period following the First World War could not sustain themselves in the face of the cruel contradictions of the 1930's: the depression (only partially solved by the New Deal); the rise of the fascist states; the Second World War, and the military use of nuclear fission and its later developments. No matter when the American people lost its innocence, the post World War II period marked the widespread recognition by the religious and other intellectuals of the dominant culture that they were not only naked, but also had been thrust out of Eden. This recognition gave rise to an intense preoccupation with theological questions, influenced in large measure by European models, most particularly Karl Barth, and the emergence of positions resolutely critical, and often less than understanding, of the liberalism of the past.

For the American Jewish community and its religious intellectuals, this development was of little consequence at the moment. Confronted by the enormity of the Jewish disaster of the 1930's and 1940's; involved in rescue and rehabilitation of the remnant; concerned with the political problems of the Palestinian community, and filled with enthusiasm at the emergence of the State of Israel and its survival, American Jews attempted no serious assessment of the intellectual structures of Jewish existence. Thus Will Herberg's *Judaism and Modern Man,* a work clearly influenced by Niebuhrian thought but also reflecting the existentialist positions of the German Jewish thinkers Martin Buber and Franz Rosenzweig, met for the most part vigorous rejection and even denunciation that had little or nothing to do with its real deficiencies. The liberalism that American Protestantism rejected, however, found a home in Jewish thought, although it was proclaimed rather than used as an intellectual instrument for examining and understanding the situation of the Jew. Even the Jewish indigenous writings of Abraham Joshua Heschel, also touched by Buber's and Rosenzweig's influence, found little response. They often were judged more by the appearance of the word "mysticism" in his academic title (he is professor of Jewish ethics and mysticism) and by his textured literary style than by the theological structure of his works.

Yet the world could not forever be held at arm's length and the intellectual environment could not be ignored. Liberal optimism could not cope with the question put by the murder of six million; nor was the singling out for destruction of the Jews as Jews to be dealt with constructively by those who understood the chosenness of Israel as a call to spiritual laureateship, or by those who found it an obsolete formulation of national genius. The reality of the State of Israel, greeted by some traditionalists as "footsteps of the Messiah," was largely unassimilable, except as a positivistically viewed political fact. Also, the influence of Buber on Protestant and, to a lesser degree, Roman Catholic thought while Jewish thinkers continued to disregard him, was somewhat more than a minor scandal in the face of his determinedly Jewish provenance and the undeniable fact that he was speaking to the situation of the Jew. In light of this intellectual situation and the sociological phenomena noted above, it is small wonder that the decade saw a growing concern of intellectuals with questions of theology.

Auschwitz Theology

It is just this optimistic reading of man's nature and situation, surreptitiously imported from idealism into pragmatism, that is rejected in its totality by a . . . singular disciple of Kaplan. Perhaps it is unwise to call Richard Rubenstein a disciple of Mordecai M. Kaplan. Yet, careful analysis of his writings [e.g., *After Auschwitz*] suggests that, in one way or another, Reconstructionism's critique of traditional and liberal positions made possible Rubenstein's development. Kaplan's people-centered interpretation of Judaism taught him that theological concepts are to be thought of basically as expressions of the community's experience, which could be demythologized and replaced by ideas presumed to be intellectually more compatible with the new situation of the community. Thus, for example, Kaplan's rejection of the concept of the chosen people was taken over by Rubenstein as a means of extricating the Jewish people from what he understands to be the consequences of "accepting the normative Judeo-Christian theology of history." Rather,

> *Religious uniqueness does not necessarily place us at the center of the divine drama of perdition, redemption, and salvation for mankind. All we need for a sure religious life is to recognize that we are, when given normal opportunities, neither more nor less than any other men, sharing*

*the pain, the joy, and the fated destiny which Earth alone has meted
out to all her children.*

Except for the final clause, the formulation is Reconstructionist in
temper. But Reconstructionism's lack of tragic vision, which, from
Rubenstein's point of view, it shares with both traditional and
liberal readings of Judaism, also makes it unsatisfactory for him as
an instrument for interpreting the Jewish and human situation. In
Auschwitz and in existentialist thought, as found in the writings of
Albert Camus, Rubenstein discovers that human existence is tragic,
ultimately hopeless, and without meaning.

Yet, since religion is the projection of the community's experience, whatever it may be, recognition of its situation allows it to
formulate a statement giving meaning to what, in itself, is meaningless. Thus, facing an ultimately absurd world, the "people of Israel,"
rejecting historicity, acts out meaning as the hieratic gesture of a
sacral community. It is, in communal terms, Camus's rejection of
suicide in the *Myth of Sisyphus.* That formulation need not begin
de novo, for, Rubenstein holds, embedded within the Jewish tradition are the recollections of just such a world-view, one overcome,
but not irretrievably, by what he calls the prophetic-Deuteronomic
theology of history: "The priests of ancient Israel," he writes, "wisely
never suffered Yahweh entirely to win his war with Baal, Astarte,
and Anath . . . Paganism was transformed but never entirely done
away with in Judaism."

Thus, when the theology-of-history superstructure is dismantled,
it will be recognized that "Almighty Necessity has never ceased Her
omnipotent reign. We are born but to perish. We are more than the
fools of the gods; we are their food . . . The Kingdom lies ahead
of us, but it is not the new reality . . . It is the Nothingness out of
which we have come and to which we are inescapably destined to
return." This, for Rubenstein, is the fundamental insight of paganism into the human situation, and such an insight, utilizing the
forms of traditional Judaism, he writes, "is the only meaningful
religious option remaining to Jews after Auschwitz and the rebirth
of Israel."

Here is the methodology of Reconstructionism, applied with a
vengeance; but here, too, is an agonizing attempt to deal with the
two crucial events of the 1940's—Auschwitz and the State of Israel—
a task barely undertaken by thinkers of more conventional positions.
Whatever responses Rubenstein called forth were marked more by
sorrow or angry repudiation than by careful analysis.

Fundamentally, Rubenstein's interpretation of the prophetic
understanding of history is far from convincing; his easy glide from
Deuteronomic to prophetic-Deuteronomic is an act of scholarly
legerdemain, illegitimately equating the cult-centered historical
thesis of Deuteronomy and its religious interests with the prophets'

nonreligious reading of Israel's history. However that may be, Rubenstein reminds us that the entwined problem of history and evil knows no easy answer. Yet the experience of the people of Israel is so intimately bound up with the problem that it is ignored at our spiritual and intellectual peril.

Joseph B. Soloveitchik

By something more than fateful coincidence, Rubenstein's interpretation of the people of Israel as a sacral community has its counter-image in, or is a counter-image for, the covenantal faith-community adumbrated by Joseph Soloveitchik in his essay, "The Lonely Man of Faith." That community, too, has its beginning in man's recognition that "he is just a handful of dust," in his "ever-growing tragic awareness of his aloneness and only-ness and consequently of his loneliness and insecurity." He, too, must "bring his quest for redemption to full realization . . . must initiate action leading to the discovery of a companion who . . . will . . . with him form a community." What is striking up to this point is the essential agreement between the two existential portraits of man in search of redemption, despite the crucial significance of the totally different way in which they are arrived at and the dissimilarity of the language used. It would be neither helpful nor constructive to continue the correlation between the two. Yet, unless this agreement is noticed at least to this point, we will fail to recognize the undeniable truth that the traditionalist *rav* and the "arch-heretic" are caught up in the same nexus of human tragedy and do their theology within the same existential framework, despite the differences in how it is done.

It is the how-ness of Soloveitchik's theology, rather than its content, that is altogether striking in contemporary Jewish thought. However, the content is not to be dismissed as unimportant, for, as presented here, it is an intellectually sophisticated and sensitively informed contemporary statement of a traditional position, commanding respectful attention. In it the twofold nature of man is examined and the kind of community emerging from each is described. It deals in detail with the tension between the two communities of man—the one, the "product of the creative, social gesture in which [man] engages whenever he thinks that collective living and acting will promote his interests"; the other, a "new kind of fellowship which one finds in the existential community" where "one lonely soul finds another soul tormented by loneliness and solitude yet unqualifiedly committed." The latter community is composed not of "two grammatical *personae*, the 'I' and the 'thou,'" but "comprises three participants: 'I, thou, and He,' the He in whom all being is rooted and in whom everything finds its rehabilitation and, consequently, redemption."

The major part of the paper provides an analysis of the covenantal faith-community created by man's surrender to the divine. In particular, Soloveitchik relates covenantal and natural man to *halakhah* [law], whose theological ramifications have loomed large in his thought and are laid down in his earlier paper, "Halakhic Man." From this vantage point he examines the situation of contemporary man who has dismissed "the covenantal faith-community as something superfluous and obsolete." This man is not a follower of "the vulgar and illiterate atheism professed and propagated in the most ugly fashion by a natural-political community which denies the unique transcendental worth of the human personality." He is "Western man who is affiliated with organized religion and is a generous supporter of its institutions. He stands today in danger of losing his dialectic awareness and of abandoning completely the metaphysical polarity implanted in man as a member of both the majestic [natural] and covenantal community." Soloveitchik is concerned here, in a fashion reminiscent of Karl Barth, with a distinction between the religious community whose "prime purpose is the successful furtherance of the interests . . . of man who values religion in terms of its usefulness to him and considers the religious act a medium through which he may increase his happiness," and "a covenantal faith community." It is from the man of culture that the man of faith takes his departure "to the abode of loneliness. . . . He experiences not only ontological loneliness but also social isolation whenever he dares to deliver the genuine faith *kerygma*. This is both the destiny and the human historical situation of the man who keeps rendezvous with eternity, and who, in spite of everything, continues tenaciously to being the message of faith to majestic man." In light of Rubenstein's question of Auschwitz, one must ask: Is this an indication of an as yet unspelled-out theological affirmation of the "sanctification of the Name" that, above and beyond all else, is the sign of the covenant community?

To turn to the matter of how Soloveitchik does theology, let us pick up the brief hint contained in the earlier reference to Karl Barth. When reading Soloveitchik, one is struck almost at once with the programmatic similarity of these two men. Essentially, they theologize out of man's existential situation, from the biblical text. Soloveitchik's paper is an extended comment on the double creation story in the early chapters of Genesis, in which the Adam of each story and the unfolding of each narrative are understood as types of man, his environment, his community. By rights, one should use the terms *drash* [homily] *midrash* [exegesis] to describe the method. But these have become so overlaid with the suggestion of homiletics, rather than searching out of the text, that their use may lead to misunderstanding.

Soloveitchik reestablished for himself, in contemporary terms, the kind of biblical exegesis that is the foundation and framework of Maimonides's *Guide of the Perplexed*. This should not suggest a similarity between his typology and the philosophical exegesis of Maimonides, but it points to the patent fact that both view the Bible as offering man in his existential plight the means of understanding his situation. What makes Soloveitchik's development and use of this way of doing theology so fascinating is the peculiar circumstance that, since the 18th century, the very *halakhic* [legal] school of which he is considered the greatest contemporary master by those capable of judging the matter has all but ignored Scripture as a foundation for a constructive statement of Judaism,—if, indeed, it concerned itself with the problem at all.

All of which leads to some concluding remarks about the so-called New Theology [See Arnold J. Wolf, ed., *Rediscovering Judaism* (Chicago, 1965)] in whose ranks the writer is a supernumerary spear-carrier. Of it, the editor wrote in his introduction: "The reader will find in this book contemporary answers to the classic problems of Jewish theology." Some critics have chided us for not having lived up to that "promise," but that was not really the "promise." What we sought was a corporate turning of intention in our approach to Jewish theology. We had each decided within ourselves, after several seasons of extended intense discussion together, that we would have to move out in a new direction if our intellectual reflection upon the tradition was to have any meaning. *Rediscovering Judaism* therefore asserts that our self-conscious standing within the tradition is the crucial center of our reflection.

This has now been most clearly articulated by Emil Fackenheim, one of the contributors to the volume. In a recent book [*Quest for Past and Future: Essays in Jewish Theology* (Bloomington and London, 1968)], and most particularly in the introductory essay, he articulates what he and the rest of us are trying to do. The importance of the statement lies in the fact that Fackenheim is a professional philosopher, bringing to the discussion the acumen and hard-headedness of his discipline. There is no confusion of categories, no hidden agenda. What the philosopher is called upon to do and the theologian seeks to accomplish are laid out without compromise. The theologian does not hide behind the philosopher's gown. He does his "thing" because it is in and of itself worth doing. He is grateful to the philosopher for his distinctions and his criticism; he accepts and uses both *in the place in which he, the theologian, stands*—and it is not the philosopher's place. Therefore, Fackenheim's essays sum up, in a significant way, the endeavor of the decade. But they do more than that; they confront the future. Fackenheim is totally aware of and sensitive to Rubenstein's double foci, Auschwitz and Israel. For him, they are the tasks for the theologian tomorrow. However, Fackenheim looks upon Rubenstein's solution as no solution at all. His own intent is to deal with the two *facts* in such a way as not to give Hitler his victory. Does he sense,

as this writer has begun to, that Rubenstein unwittingly may be
doing just that? At any rate, Fackenheim must now be seen as the
theological mentor of the last and, we may hope, the next decade,
for a significant segment of the nontraditionalist community.

What connects the writings of the men of the New Theology
with those of a Rubenstein (who may indeed turn out to be purely
idiosyncratic) and Rabbi Soloveitchik is a sense of urgency whose
existential nature is not just one emerging from the general human
condition, but from the particularly Jewish. Perhaps it is precisely
this point that differentiates Jewish theological endeavor from the
Christian, and makes conversation so difficult or easily misunder-
stood. The Christian theologian seems to begin his explanation
from his being man, not Christ-man, Christian having no ontic
status. The Jew begins with his being Jew-man, not just man, Jew
having ontic status. Existentially, it is reflection upon the whatness
and how-ness of being Jew that has set in motion the otherwise
diverse programs and positions we have discussed.

Put yet another way, it may be said that the dominant tone of
this decade's Jewish doing of theology has been confessional. This
clearly emerges from Fackenheim's response to the recent and, I
suspect, ephemeral trend in American Protestant theology, gathered
under the unhelpful labels "Death of God" or "World Come of
Age":

> *The Jew is singled out for special contradictions. In America he enjoys
> a freedom and security unparalleled in his history; yet he is but twenty
> years separated from the greatest and as yet uncomprehended Jewish
> catastrophe. His trust and joy in the modern-secular world cannot but
> coexist with radical distrust and profound sorrow. Authentic Jewish
> religious witness in this age must both face up to Auschwitz and yet
> refuse a despair of this world which, wholly contrary to Judaism, would
> hand still another victory to the forces of radical evil. Insofar as he is
> committed to Jewish survival, the Jew has already taken a stand against
> these forces. But survival-for-survival's sake is an inadequate stand. The
> Jew can go beyond it only if he can reopen the quest of Jeremiah and
> Job, who for all their agony refused to despair either of God or the
> world.*[3]

Eugene B. Borowitz states that:

The most revealing occurrence in Jewish thought during the
1960's was the complete rejection of death-of-God theology. It was
totally unforeseen. The American Jewish community would have
appeared to be the religious group most highly predisposed to
accept the new radicalism. Poll after poll of the religious beliefs and
practices of Americans had shown Jews as high in agnosticism as

---

[3] Lou H. Silberman, "Concerning Jewish Theology in North America: Some Notes
on a Decade," *American Jewish Yearbook*, LXX (1969), 37–38, 39–41, 48–52, 56–57.

they were low in weekly worship. The old, rich, immigrant style of Jewish life has almost faded from memory, and passage into the majority is easier today, for it can be made through ethical humanism rather than Christian baptism. The Jews, therefore, were expected to find the announcement of the death of God an articulation of their deepest intuition and unconscious longing. Nothing of the sort happened. If anything, once the sensation wore off, the idea tended to produce the opposite result. In contrast to their pious grandparents, most Jews considered themselves unbelievers. But when called to rally to the ensign of atheism or "God as Nothing," they could not. Rather, they began to realize how much they still affirmed. The discovery of the decade was that despite a religiosity more social than existential, the Jewish community had not deserted its ancient commitments.

This development is easiest to understand if one notes the particular Jewish setting of the issue. What first moved the Jewish community was not the skeptical articles or speeches of the early 1960's, but the founding of an atheist congregation. Much earlier, at the turn of the century, Jews had given up their religion by creating and joining the ethical culture movement. Because their hidden agenda was to escape their minority status as Jews, they developed what they thought was a purely universal institution. The modern Jewish atheists were less self-deceiving. They had no desire to hide their Jewishness. If anything, they wanted to benefit from its ethnic riches, not the least of which is the way in which Jewish folkways tend to demand and motivate humane existence on every level. An atheistic Jewish congregation seemed so logical an expression of what many Jews had been saying about themselves that many people expected that a series of such congregations and a small movement would soon appear. They did not. A meticulous observer might find another such congregation in one spot or another. That would be about all. The cynical explanation would be: one can easily be a nonbeliever in the existing system, so it is not worth bothering to change. There is some truth in that statement. Yet, American Jewry, for all it may be accused of, is hardly that hypocritical and dishonest.

Among Jews, such theology as exists is as much a function of the experience of the people of Israel itself as it is of professors or other intellectuals. Even in biblical times, the prophets and historians were largely critics of what the Israelite folk did. To this, they brought the judgment and teaching of God. In ages of lesser inspiration, though formulation is important, Judaism is essentially shaped by the Jewish community in the full dimensions of its religio-ethnic existence. Jewish theology is always a response to Jewish history, more statically in the Middle Ages, more actively today.

Once that is clear, the interpretation of what happened in the 1960's follows directly, though it is as ironic in impact as it seems illogical in deduction. The historic facts are obvious enough. The result of the Holocaust was not a massive Jewish defection from God. Nor was there a flight from Jewish identity, though that inevitably carries with it the overtones of Covenant. To the contrary, the overwhelming majority of concentration-camp survivors . . . did not think twice about deserting the people of Israel. Despite what they had been through, they picked up their Jewish existence, mostly with a new sense of self-determination and seriousness. The State of Israel is one result of that new mood of Jewishness. Though it was born as much out of necessity as of resolve, the mixture is not atypical of the Jewish understanding of the operations of Providence. One cannot understand the State of Israel today or the relations of world Jewry to it, unless one realizes the elemental nature of the decisions after Auschwitz: there will be no more Holocausts; the Jewish people must live!

World Jewry, too, despite decades of Jewish atheism and nonobservance, did not seek, either by apathy or by active assimilation, to escape the new sense of Jewish destiny. There may be serious complaints against the quality of Jewish life everywhere, but the very standards by which the negative judgments are made are higher now than they were a generation ago or even during the days of Hitler. The ironic fact has been that the Holocaust, which should have dispirited and demoralized the Jews, made an aimless generation realize it must be true to its Jewishness.

A New Commandment Sounds

Emil Fackenheim, who has done the most penetrating Jewish analysis of the philosophical defects of death-of-God thinking, has given this Jewish response what seems already to have become classic utterance. From the midst of the destruction, the Jewish people has heard a command that it knew must be heeded: the survival of the Jews is now an ultimate value. For Jewry to die, or even decline, would be to give Hitler the victory. The Jews may not give Hitler in death what he was denied in life. To the traditional 613 commandments, there is now added a 614th: thou shalt preserve and maintain, enhance, and enrich the life of the Jewish people.

That does not mean that the Jews see God as He speaks from Auschwitz. No, in the midst of that overwhelming evil they cannot perceive He-who-commands. But they hear the commandment sound with all the ultimacy that they have heard before in a tradition that goes back to Sinai. And, because they are the people of Israel, bound to an unending Covenant, they have now, as then, found the strength to accept and follow it.

Fackenheim does not claim that this is an answer to the question of Auschwitz, but he is too good a Jew not to know an authentic Jewish response when he sees one. He is doing theology out of the living religious experience of the Jewish people. The Jewish theologian's proper task is not to decide *a priori* the possibility or validity of such experience but, when he recognizes an event as genuine, to do what he can to give it cognitive illumination. The community, in due course, acknowledges who are its proper teachers.

So the professors' problems with God . . . have not had much effect upon the minority of thoughtful Jews. Some do find it challenging that contemporary linguistic philosophy finds God-talk peculiar and, within the constricted meaning that it gives to meaning, largely meaningless. Others are somewhat intrigued that the students of Whitehead's student Hartshorne have now come to maturity and are trying to revive metaphysics. Neither the absent God of the former nor the abstract God of the latter had made much impact on the Jewish mind. These formulations yield, at best, a God for the academic community, with its highly refined problems. What Jews care about is a God for history, and, in particular, one who has something to do with the real experience of the Jewish people. If Jews were to mourn God's death, it would be because of the suffering under Hitler, not because of philosophic incoherence, as some theoretician redefines it.

Another Event to Cope With

That realization left most American Jews and their representative thinkers in a state of suspended formulation, working only out of a theology of non-nonbelief. That state was, however, shaken by another experience of the Jewish people: The Arab-Israeli six-day war of June 1967. In the weeks from the closing of the Straits of Tiran to the outbreak of the war, there were so many Arab threats of another Holocaust that Jews around the world grew daily more anxious and depressed—a condition aggravated by the nations of the world, who, it seemed to most Jews, did little to stop the war but, in effect, once again abandoned a Jewish community to destruction. When the Israeli victory came, and came with such suddenness, there was among Jews, for a moment, a sense of the genuine presence of God in history once again. Today, that is something of an intellectual embarrassment. Then it was unquestionably real and almost universally felt. It did not answer Auschwitz. Nothing could. But it made personally clear that God was not always absent from individuals and peoples, though His saving power surely functioned unfathomably. Before the Temple's Western Wall in Jerusalem, most Jewish agnostics prayed first and rationalized it later. . . .

The Existentialist Circle

The most easily identifiable form that this has taken is the theological consensus which has emerged among a group of thinkers, men largely in their forties. They stand in sharp disagreement with Mordecai M. Kaplan, the most distinguished thinker of the World War II period. They are respectful of the intellectual accomplishment, and admire the moral leadership, of Abraham J. Heschel who came to prominence in the 1950's. However, they are not his disciples, but tend to derive their position by moving forward from the style and ideas of the Jewish existentialists Franz Rosenzweig and Martin Buber. Their position is somewhat difficult to expound because no full-scale works have been authored by men of this circle. The critical points would seem to be the acceptance of some form of revelation, generally Buberian, on the part of the liberals, and a concern with belief as a matter of personal appropriation on the part of the traditionalists. These motifs find expression in all the old Jewish theological concerns—commandment, law, sin, atonement— but particularly in the unique Jewish relationship with God, the Covenant between Him and the people of Israel, which gives context to all else in Judaism.

Where Are the People Going?

They are partly responding to, partly trying to lead forward, the positive side of American Jewish life. For all the continuing, lugubrious comments about the future of the Jewish community, there is a discernible faithfulness to its direction. There has been no recent shortage of candidates for the rabbinate; most seminaries report that the quality of their candidates is quite high. Many more men do come there to go on to teach, but the revival of Jewish study as a way of life, and the prospect of a large number of college students who have had a sophisticated introduction to Judaism, is exciting. Besides, the overwhelming majority of rabbinical students is interested in congregational work and rather well informed about what awaits it. Defections from the rabbinate to other areas of activity may be slightly higher than in previous years, and rabbinic morale is a worry, but these problems comprise nothing like the state of emergency which one hears about elsewhere. There is some research to indicate that the gap between Jewish parents and teenagers is less great than it was a generation ago when the immigrant-native-born conflict racked most Jewish families. There is good reason to believe that, regardless of theologies as yet unborn, the American Jewish community in ten years will be more like than unlike what it is today.

The most intriguing signs of change are seen in the increasing severity of judgment against the American society. The 1960's have disillusioned many a sensitive American. American Jews now feel sufficiently secure to join in expressing their disappointment in our country's morality. That has engendered two tiny and unexpected developments. The one is a serious return to Judaism by young people desirous of rooting their alienation from a-ethical, exploitative Americanism in something which will give them the impetus and stamina to go about bettering it. Here the minority and nonconformist character of Judaism becomes a virtue after years of being considered a handicap. Linked with the old Jewish passion for a just and merciful society, Jewish faith now becomes a personal option for some of the most humanly gifted in the community. Another handful now finds it possible to immigrate to the State of Israel. They believe that their very presence there as part of a socially concerned, but externally embattled community will give their lives a purpose that it lacks in the American megalopolis. For the first time, the number of American Jews becoming Israelis is not negligible.

What is not visible on the horizon is a rebellion against what threatens in the next decade to become an existentialist theological establishment. There are occasional protests by young analysts or phenomenologists that a more rationally structured Judaism is required to meet the challenges of modernity. Any such development would be valuable, if only to stimulate the intelligent sort of controversy through which ideas and options are clarified. At the moment, however, the level of the questioning has rarely reached academic adequacy, being content, for the most part, to address itself to laymen or the clergy rather than to speak to the learned public. In that respect, one may say that there is a serious lack in present-day Jewish thought.

The truth may well be that the period of Jewish theological concern which developed after World War II is now moving to fruition, but without creating a new generation of intellectual offspring, either directly or in rebellion. The eyes of most younger men seem more directed to what can be done, rather than to why to do it or to what end. Can worship be made meaningful? Is it possible to educate adults or youth? How can the synagogue be a place of community as well as of activity? What should a rabbi be today? What does it mean to live a modern Jewish life? In the hands of the young radicals who are emerging from revolutionizing college education and now are battling their way through seminary, these old troubles become creative challenges. The theological shift of mood of the 1960's is almost certainly the intellectual father of that new experimentation with forms. That the fresh seed prefers to change life rather than to construct systems should probably, then, be considered not so much a rejection of Jewish theology as a desire to put it to work.[4]

[4] Eugene B. Borowitz, "Jewish Theology Faces the 1970's," *The Annals of the American Academy of Political and Social Science,* CCCLXXXVII (January, 1970), 23, 24–26, 26–28, 28–29.

Like Zionism, contemporary Judaic theology vividly portrays a paradox: the persistence of the archaic, the predominance of the modern. The whole agenda of Judaic theology, the range of proof-texts, the authorities whose opinions are supposed to register—these derive from the religious record of pre-modern Judaism. But the formulation of issues and mode of argumentation, the resort to philosophic modes of discourse, and the effort to address the dilemmas of faith facing modern Jews—these obviously reflect a new world, and a secular one, in which no one takes for granted what in ages past everyone knew to be true.

That is not to suggest that theology in the modern mode—the effort to address believers and unbelievers, Jew and Gentile, through a common language of argument—is without precedent. At those points in the history of Judaism when Jews lived as they do today, in the midst of Gentiles whose culture they respected and whose language they spoke, one finds the development of philosophical theology. Philo's Alexandria, Saadia's Baghdad, Maimonides' Spain and Egypt, like Silberman's and Borowitz's America, all produced men who sought a way to a religious understanding of the world. What separates American from earlier theologians of Judaism is what stands between America and the modern West, on the one side, and pre-modern times on the other: the capacity for belief, the routineness of religious conviction, then everywhere commonplace, now rare and attained only after anguished struggle.

What is remarkable about contemporary Judaic theology in America is not its achievements, but the fact that it exists at all. It testifies to the need of modern men to stand apart from and to criticize their convictions, whether supernatural or otherwise. It is in the end the best evidence of the modernity of modern men: their acute self-consciousness, their utter incapacity ever again wholly and unselfconsciously to participate in tradition—any tradition.

chapter 6

ARCHAIC AND MODERN, SACRED AND SECULAR

HOW SHALL WE INTERPRET the materials before us? Is American Judaism the disorganized remnant of a tradition once integrated, now in a shambles, degenerate and hopeless of reformation and reconstruction, at best capable of survival like a fossil? Or do we discern something fundamentally different from its antecedents, not decayed but regenerate, the courageous response of vital people to the new and challenging situation of modernity?

The answer depends not upon facts, on which all may agree, but on the interpretation of the facts, on judgment. For American Judaism sharply poses the enigma of religion in post-archaic times: What do we understand by "religion" after the collapse of classical myth and the end of old modes of believing? If the old stands as stern judge of all to follow, then the verdict is clear. But if what is different may legitimately claim both to be new and to possess its own integrity, then only the future will tell what is decayed or what is regenerate.

Modern men, among them Jews, sentimentally speak of sacred revelation, but they live by secular enlightenment. They speak of the voice of God, through revealed Torah guiding every action from Heaven, lending supernatural significance to trivial, commonplace matters. But they live by simple rules of accepted conduct. They read the works of prophecy, but discover knowledge through research. They fantasize about the *shtetl,* the ideal cathectic life of the corporate community. But by choice they live in the great, anomic cities of America. They profess a parochial culture and prefer endogamy. But they stand in the vanguard of international culture, in which appeals to singular revelation carry less weight then the demands of reason, and by which parochialism and self-verifying realms of discourse and meaning are set aside in favor of a single, universal language of thought and technology.

If you agree that these traits characterize the modern and secular, not the archaic and sacred, then you must first of all wonder how modern is the process of modernization, for it is as old as the Greeks. In the process of the Hellenization of the Near East, which took place place between the fifth and third centuries B.C., we discern many of the traits we associate with modernization. Morton Smith writes: [1]

> The contrast commonly drawn between the Greek cities and the Semitic countryside has been exaggerated. The countryside was permeated by Greek elements and influences.

We refer to the internationalization of culture. Smith states:

> Typically, Greek artifacts and techniques were everywhere in use. The country [Palestine] had a monetary economy, foreign trade was a major concern, the frame of thought had ceased to be the land of Palestine and become the civilized world, and Greek had become the normal language of business and politics.

One needs only to substitute English for Greek to have an approximate description of any of the newly modern countries of Africa or Asia or of the newly modern Jews of early twentieth-century America. Smith comments:

> The forces which produced the changes called Hellenization were not universally or even primarily Greek. . . . Hellenization cannot be described simply as adoption of Greek ways by peoples of the Near East and Oriental ways by Greeks. Instead we have a vast tissue of change in which innumerable strands of independent but parallel development are interwoven with a woof of influence and reaction to produce a single new culture, the Hellenistic, which is no less different from classical Greek culture than from the cultures of the more ancient Near East.

[1] Morton Smith,*The Formation of Palestinian Judaism* (New York: Columbia University Press, 1971).

These modulations, from the classical Greek to the Hellenistic ambiance, include change in classical land tenure patterns, from the small holding-farm to the development of vast estates of king or temple; change from the small and homogeneous city-state to the absolute monarchy holding vast territories and governing various peoples; change from a way of life governed by local custom and tradition to the growth of explicit, written laws, derived not from revelation or tradition but from legislation and rational assessment of current needs; change from a religion in which the cult of the gods of the city was the center for petition and patriotism to the universal cult of a divine ruler without political affiliations; change from a situation in which private individuals mattered and politics was an important concern, to one in which political units were so enormous that nonpolitical arts and philosophy, centering upon the private affairs of radically isolated individuals, became the focus of the individual life; change from the civil administration by amateurs to the development of professional bureaucracies; and finally, change from cultic religion to metaphysical philosophy.

In Palestine, as elsewhere in the Middle East, the passage from traditional culture to international, Hellenistic culture produced, among other things, both Christianity and rabbinic Judaism. Neither Western religious tradition derives from the Hebrew Scriptures, the Old Testament. In their own times both were "modern" and stood upon the interpretation of the Hebrew Scriptures supplied by men who lived in a world as different from that of ancient Israel—five or six centuries earlier—as the modern world is different from the world of medieval Christendom and classical Judaism. So those who would judge the construction of American Judaism as merely degenerate must issue a similar verdict upon the works of those who laid the foundations for the tradition recently so radically revised in America. Whoever prefers the simple and Hellenic to the sophisticated and Hellenistic, the classic to the complex, and the old to the new, will ratify that judgment.

Clearly, what happens to archaic religious forms in modern times reveals change, and not all change is for the better. But the real problem is, What do those changes tell us about the condition of modern man, the challenges that confront him, his responses to them?

American Jews half a century ago would not have claimed "religious" as an appropriate adjective for their community. Today they insist upon it. The moralists' criticism of religion will always render ever more remote what is meant by "true religion," so we need not be detained by carping questions. But can there be religion with so minimal a quotient of supernatural experience, theological conviction, and evocative ritual, including prayer, as is revealed in American Judaism? If one draws the dividing line between belief in a supernatural God and atheism, then much of American Jewry, also much of American Judaism, may stand on the far side of that line. If the dividing line is, in the words of Krister Stendahl, "between the closed mind and spiritual sensibility and imagination," then American Jews and American Judaism may stand within the frontier of the religious, the sacred.

Let us begin with the substitution of organizations and group activity for a holy way of life lived by each individual. What the Jews have done in their revision of the holy way is to conform to, in their own way to embody, the American talent at actually accomplishing things. Americans organize. They do so not to keep themselves busy, but to accomplish efficiently and with an economy of effort a great many commendable goals. They hire "professionals" to do well what most individuals cannot do at all: heal the sick, care for the needy, tend the distressed at home and far away. In modern society people do not keep guns in their homes for self-protection. They have police. Nations do not rely upon the uncertain response of well-meaning volunteers. They form armies. The things American Jews seek to accomplish through their vast organizational life derive, as Weisberg admits, from their tradition: They want to educate the young and old, to contribute to the building of the ancient land, to see to it that prayers are said and holidays observed. Now hiring a religious virtuoso may seem less commendable than saying one's own prayers, but it is merely an extension of the specialization people take for granted elsewhere.

In archaic times people believed that salvation depended upon keeping to the holy way, so each person kept to it, made himself sufficiently expert to know how to carry out the law. Today few believe that supernatural salvation inheres in prayers, dietary taboos, and Sabbath observance. It is therefore curious that the Jews nonetheless want to preserve the old salvific forms and symbols, as they certainly do. Few pray. Fewer still believe in prayer. It is astonishing that the synagogues persist in focusing their collective life upon liturgical functions. Perhaps the best analogy is to a museum, in which old art is preserved and displayed, though people do not paint that way any more, may not even comprehend what the painter did, the technical obstacles he overcame. The synagogue is a living museum and preserves the liturgical and ritual life of the old tradition. Why should Jews choose this way, when earlier in their American experience they seemed to move in a different direction? Is it nostalgia for a remembered, but unavailable experience of the sacred? Is the religious self-definition they have adopted merely an accommodation to American expectations? Or do they hope the archaic and the supernatural may continue to speak to them?

The figure of the rabbi calls forth the same wonderment. Why call

oneself "rabbi" at all, if one is not a saint, a scholar, a judge? Given the
ultimate mark of secularization—the complaint that rabbis no longer
reach high places in the Jewish community—should we not ask, What is
still sacred in the rabbi and his learning, calling, leadership? The answer
would be, nothing whatsoever, were it not for the testimony of Rubenstein's account, which rings true to my ears, of peoples' relationships to
the rabbi, their fantastic expectations of him. The absurd, pathetic,
posturing rabbi, without adequate education for his tasks, unsure of his
role, at once self-isolated and complaining at his loneliness—whatever he
is, he is the rabbi. He knows it. The people know it. They look to him as
a kind of holy man. No nostalgia here: The rabbi is a completely American
adaptation of the ancient rabbinic role. But American society never imposed the peculiar, mainly secular definition of "Jewish clergyman" upon
the modern rabbi. For two hundred years American Jewry had no rabbis
at all. And the rabbis they now have are not merely Judaic versions of
Protestant ministers or Roman Catholic priests, but uniquely Judaic as
well as exceptionally American. The remembrance of rabbis of past times
—of the saints, scholars, and holy men of Europe—hardly persists into
the fourth generation and beyond. The rabbi, profane and secular, is the
only holy man they shall ever know. So onto him they fix their natural,
human fantasies about men set apart by and for God.

The holy people, "Israel," of times past has become "the American
Jewish community," uncertain what is Jewish about itself, still more
unsure of what "Jewish" ought to mean at all. Surely the lingering crisis
of self-definition, characteristic of modern men in many situations, marks
the Jew as utterly modern and secular. Add to that the second component
of the holy people's self-understanding: concern for what the Gentiles
think of Jews, readiness to admit that negative opinion into the Jewish
assessment of the Jews. This submission to universal opinions and values
hardly characterizes a holy people, set apart from all others. Frail and
uncomfortable, hating those "Jewish traits" in oneself that set Jews apart
from everyone else, and wanting to be Jewish but not too much, not so
much that they cannot also be undifferentiated Americans—is this the
holy people that traversed 35 centuries of human history, proud, tenacious,
alone? Can such men as these, unable to agree on anything, be called a
people? Can they claim their collectivity to be holy, separate and apart?

Surely in the passage from the sacred to the secular, the holy people has
disintegrated, become a random group of discrete, scarcely similar individuals. Yet while that may seem to be so, the one point Jews affirm is that
they shall be Jews. This they have in common.

And their affirmation comes with such intensity and spiritual force
that one wonders what can be its source? A random collection of people,
with merely memories in common (and that seems to me spurious senti-

mentality at best), or who suppose they share a common fate (which is rare), or who imagine and fear a common tragedy (which is meretricious) —such a group ought not pugnaciously to affirm its collective existence as do the Jews. The very vigor of their activity together and the commonalities of a quite discrete folk suggest that the group, once a people, is still a people. The secular separateness of the Jews, their inner awareness of being a group, their outward view of themselves as in some ways apart from others—that separateness is probably all modern man can hope for socially to approximate "the holy." The archaic "holy people" has passed from the scene. In its place stands something different in all respects but the most important: its manifest and correct claim to continue as Jews, a different, separate group, *and* the claim that that difference is destiny.

Of the complex relationship between secular Zionism and sacred messianism, modern nation building and the myth of the return to Zion at the end of time, I have already said enough. It seems clear that the pattern I claim to discern recurs, perhaps most vividly, in the modern and secular modulation of the myth of the holy land.

Concerning holy Torah we asked three questions: What of the religious life of American Jews? What of the study of Torah? And what of the theological enterprise?

The first question produces an uninteresting answer, the second, an obvious one. But the third is consequential: The grandsons of Jews who would not have understood what theologians do, but persisted in an episodic, aphoristic expression of a folk faith as theology enough, not only write theology, but correctly claim it to be Judaic. This is the decisive evidence that something new has been created out of something old: Contemporary American Judaism, for all its distance from the classic forms of the past, its unbelief and secularity, constitutes a fundamentally new and autonomous development, not merely the last stages in the demise of something decadent.

American Judaism calls forth, in the task of formulating a systematic account of its faith, the talents of men of philosophical sophistication and religious conviction, able to speak in the name, even in the words, of the classic tradition, but in a language alien to that tradition. To be sure, we devoted little attention to the Judaic theological enterprise, but that seemed appropriate, for the Jews' response to Judaic theology thus far is routine and inconsequential. The best books reach a tiny audience, the worst only a slightly larger one. The finest theological journals are read chiefly by those who write for them, or aspire to. So the theological movement must stand by itself, as evidence of the modernity and secularity of the theologians, on the one side, but of their participation in the traditional sacred values and in the archaic texts, on the other.

I argue, therefore, that American Judaism constitutes something more than the lingering end of olden ways and myths. It is the effort of modern men to make use of archaic ways and myths for the formation of a religious way of living appropriate to an unreligious time and community. Spiritual sensibility and, even more, the remnants of the archaic imagination are the sources for the unarticulated, but evident decision of American Jews to reconstruct out of the remnants of an evocative, but incongruous heritage the materials of a humanly viable, meaningful community life. To have attempted the reconstitution of traditional villages in the metropolis and of archaic ways of seeing the world in the center of modernity would have been to deny the human value and pertinence of the tradition itself. But few wanted even to try. In the end the effort would have had no meaning. The Jews were men who had the courage to insist that life— their life together—must have more than ordinary meaning. In American Judaism they embarked upon the uncertain quest to find, if necessary to invent, to build that meaning. Despite their failures, the gross, grotesque form they have imposed upon the old tradition, that uncommon, courageous effort seems to me to testify to whatever is good and enduring in modernity. But whether good or not, abiding or ephemeral, all that modern men have, and all that they shall ever have, is the mature hope to persist in that quest.

EPILOGUE

WHAT WE HAVE DONE is to assemble a rich array of materials without significantly contributing to the theoretical understanding of modernity or post-archaic religion. To make such a contribution, we should have had to formulate more supple, less mechanical interpretations of our central categories of inquiry. Modern and modernity, sacred, archaic, classical, secular, religious—all of these terms have been used as if I had given to them precise definitions; however, I have not. You therefore cannot be satisfied with our present interpretation of the complex materials of American Judaism, for, having presented a repertoire of data, I cannot claim to have accomplished the hermeneutical task at all, or even to have attempted it. I should argue, however, that a far wider selection of data, drawn from the religious situation of many sorts of modern men, is required for that purpose. The Jews may prove in the end merely suggestive, but by no means definitive, of the experience of modernity.

For we legitimately ask whether American Judaism, or at least its modern, non-orthodox sectors, may at all be regarded as an essentially valid datum for the study of American religions. Clearly the Jews constitute a well-demarcated ethnic community. But, among such disproportionately small numbers of Jews, is a persistent religious perspective upon themselves and upon life sufficient to characterize them all as a religious group? The process of modernization has not merely rendered their group life more complex and varied, but also seems to have obliterated from their group life the last remnants of a religious way of viewing reality. Many have lost sight of the full implications of the religious language and symbolism of the classic Judaic tradition. They scarcely make use of religious symbols to relate themselves to the conditions of their existence. Such symbols as survive scarcely relate to the conditions of group—much less individual—existence. American Jews cannot claim to apprehend the symbolic or mythic structure of traditional Judaism or of its modern developments in the way Bellah suggests: "Through religious symbols man has symbolized to himself his own identity and the order of existence in terms of which his identity makes sense." [1] If one substitutes "Jewishness" for "religious symbols," then we have no discontinuity, for American Jews in the main do identify themselves in large measure through "being Jewish." But since the substance of "Jewishness" contains little of transcendent meaning, can it be regarded as other than of merely cultural and sociological, but not religious, interest?

Where is the human anguish, joy, tragedy, mystery, or awe in American Judaism? Where the sense of the sacred? Where the vision? Bellah cites Wilfred C. Smith: "A religious symbol is successful if men can express in terms of it the highest and deepest vision of which they are capable, and if in terms of it that vision can be nourished and can be conveyed to others within one's group." [2] Do American Jews possess any such symbol, profess such a faith as to lead to a vision beyond the mundane data of their very worldly group life? That seems to me the central dilemma facing American Judaism: Its commitment to the rationality, respectability, and worldliness of the middle-class life to which Jews aspire, and in large part have achieved, seems to conflict with the vision contained in the holy books and deeds, indeed, with the whole symbolic structure of the Judaic inheritance. When the theologians have had their say, they still have not drawn the transcendent thorn from the rational rose—and transcendence, supernaturalism, reference to salvation and the eschaton, things not of this world—these seem the perquisites, in some form or other, of the religious quest for meaning.

Perhaps Judaism is actually disfunctional, because both its classic and its contemporary forms (and they are not so far apart) may not provide a secure, stable foundation for the collective life of the American Jews. So far as the Jews build that life solely upon this-worldly considerations, they render religious expression either irrelevant, or meretricious, or merely sentimental. But so soon as they speak of themselves in mythic language

1 Robert Bellah, *Beyond Belief* (New York: Harper and Row, Publishers, 1970), p. 195.
2 *Ibid.*, p. 204.

and respond to the existential challenge in accord with the Judaic response, they repudiate the worldliness, the confidence, the practicality of their present group life, for they thereby abandon their pugnacious secularity.

Which, then: ethnic group or religious community? If the former, why? If the latter, how? Individuals in the ethnic group are bound to raise religious questions, and if the answers do not come from Judaism, they will come from somewhere else—and this the ethnic group cannot endure. The religious community, however, is bound to exclude some in its commitment to a vision and symbolic structure, and the Jews have been wise in not excluding anyone born into their group, whatever his vision.

This disintegration of the archaic religious and ethnic unity of the "holy people" seems to me the most important Judaic testimony about what it means to be a modern man. But the story of the tension between the ethnic datum of Jewish group life and the religious critique and interpretation of that group life constitutes most of the history of Judaism. If so, the modern age brings new evidence of an astonishing continuity.

SUGGESTIONS FOR FURTHER READING

THE READER MUST WONDER what has become of the standard facts of the history of American Jews and American Jewry, for we have concentrated upon a different sort of data. So the first thing he will want to do is to sort out what happened, in proper sequence. By far the best accounts of the Jews and the Jewish religion in America, their institutions, beliefs, and historical development, are Nathan Glazer, *American Judaism* (Chicago: University of Chicago Press, 1957) and Moshe Davis, "Jewish Religious Life and Institutions in America (A Historical Study)," in Louis Finkelstein, ed., *The Jews: Their History, Culture, and Religion* (New York: Harper and Row, Publishers, 1960 [3]), I, 488–587. A factual, popular history of American Jews is Rufus Learsi, *The Jews in America* (Cleveland: World, 1954). On contemporary American Jews, two sociological works provide a good beginning, Charles Bezalel Sherman, *The Jew within American Society, A Study in Ethnic Individuality* (Detroit: Wayne State University Press, 1961), and Marshall Sklare, ed., *The Jews: Social Patterns of an American Group* (New York: Free Press of Glencoe, 1958), a collection of excellent essays on the whole range of sociological and historical problems. Every topic treated here may be further explored in the essays collected by Sklare.

Since these are merely suggestions for further reading, not a bibliography— Davis and Glazer provide good introductions to bibliographical questions—I may add a reference to two further works of my own, which focus in different ways upon the issues raised in this book. *The Way of Torah: An Introduction to Judaism* (Encino: Dickenson, 1970) introduces the mythic structure of classical

Judaism and traces continuities and changes in modern times, of which the American Judaism is only one part. In *Babylonian Judaism in Talmudic Times* (Nashville: Abingdon, 1971) are treated the problems of power, myth, and function in the classical period of the history of Judaism. The former supplies the context for the consideration of the modernity of American Judaism. The latter draws the contrast between a community fully within the classical myth and expressive of the power relationships explained by that myth, on the one side, and the modern structure of American Jewry and its religion, on the other.

In *The Way of Torah* are many other suggestions for reading on Judaism. Among these, I especially recommend James Michener, *The Source* (New York: Random House, 1965), and Herman Wouk, *This Is My God* (New York: Doubleday, 1959), as practically painless ways to learn about the whole history of the Jews and about modern Orthodox Judaism, respectively, and Ludwig Lewisohn, *The Island Within* (Philadelphia: Jewish Publication Society, 1968), a novel which testifies to the nature and meaning of Jewish existence in America.

Theology has been sorely neglected here. A brilliant account of modern Judaic theology is Arthur A. Cohen, *The Natural and Supernatural Jew: An Historical and Theological Introduction* (New York: McGraw-Hill, 1962). The single most sophisticated, profound, and comprehensive statement *within* modern Judaic theology is Abraham J. Heschel, *God in Search of Man: A Philosophy of Judaism* (Philadelphia: Jewish Publication Society, 1956). On the relationships between Judaism and Christianity, an astringent and healthy critique is Arthur A. Cohen, *The Myth of the Judeo-Christian Tradition* (New York: Harper and Row, 1970).

GLOSSARY

GLOSSARY

Ahad HaAm "One of the People," pen name of Asher Ginzberg, 1856–1927, Zionist philosopher

Akiba Talmudic rabbi, ca. 70–135 A.D.

Aliyah lit.: Ascent, refers to immigration to the State of Israel

Bar Mitzvah Ceremony marking the assumption of religious obligations by thirteen-year-old boy

Basel Swiss city where Zionist movement was founded in 1897

B.C.E. Before the Common Era, sometimes used in place of B.C.

Bialik, Chaim Nahman Modern Hebrew poet, 1873–1934

C.E. Common Era, sometimes used in place of A.D.

Cohen, Hermann German neo-Kantian philosopher, rationalist interpreter of Judaism, 1842–1918

Diaspora Dispersion

Dubnow, Simon East European Jewish historian, ideologist, 1860–1941

Elijah, Gaon of Vilna Outstanding Talmudic scholar and ascetic, 1720–1797

Galut Exile, situation of estrangement

Geiger, Abraham Founder of reform Judaism, scholar, 1810–1874

Golah Diaspora

Golus Yiddish pronunciation for *galut*

Gordon, A.D. Nature-mystic, Zionist ideologist, 1856–1922

Goy, pl. goyim   Gentile, alien, outsider

Halakhah   Law, the way things are done

Halevi, Judah   Hebrew mystic, philosopher, poet, 1080–1141

Hanukkah   Festival of Lights, in December, celebrating Maccabees victory over Hellenists, purification of Temple from idolatry, in 165 B.C.

Hasid   Follower of Hasidism

Hasidism   Religious and mystical revival movement in 18th C. Poland and Ukraine

Herzl, Theodore   Author of *The Jewish State* (1894) and founder of modern Zionist movement, 1860–1904

Hess, Moses   Author of *Rome and Jerusalem* (1862) and early Jewish nationalist, 1812–1875

Hillel   Talmudic rabbi who taught, "What is hateful to yourself do not do to your fellow-man," d. ca. 10 A.D.

Israel Baal Shem Tov   Baal Shem Tov means master of the good name, miracle-worker; founder of Hasidism, c. 1700–1760

Jewishness   'Being Jewish,' traits associated with Jews as an ethnic group, as distinguished from *Judaism,* body of doctrines, beliefs, symbols, actions characteristic of Judaic religious tradition

Kabbalah   Judaic mystical tradition

Kashrus   Yiddish pronunciation of *Kashrut*

Kashrut   Jewish dietary laws

Kaddish   Doxology used as memorial prayer for dead

Kosher   Fit, acceptable, proper; often used for food, but applies to any aspect of daily life

Lazarus, Emma   American poet and early Zionist, 1849–1887

Luftmensch   Man with no certain means of earning a living, lives 'in air'; very spiritual person

Lulav   Palm branch, used in celebration of *Sukkot*

Maimonides, Moses   Medieval Judaic theologian, author of *Guide of the Perplexed,* 1135–1204

Maskil   *Illuminé,* enlightened person, 18th C. critics of religious gullibility and primitivism

Mitzvah, pl. mitzvot   lit.: Commandment, religious action

Minyan   Quorum, ten men; more broadly, public worship

Morenu   Our master, our teacher

Moshe Rabbenu   Moses our rabbi, master

Noah, Mordecai Manuel   American politician, journalist, philanthropist, tried to found a Jewish state, Ararat, on land near Buffalo, N.Y. in 1825; 1785–1851

Philo   Hellenistic-Judaic theologian, lived in Alexandria, 25 B.C.–40 A.D.

Rachmonis   Pity, charity

Rosenzweig, Franz German existential philosopher and theologian, wrote *Star of Redemption;* 1886–1929

Saadia Theologian, author of *Book of Beliefs and Opinions,* lived in Baghdad, wrote in Arabic and Hebrew; 882–942

Shabbat Sabbath

Shule Synagogue

Shtetl Village

Sitting *shivah* Observing period of mourning for seven *(shivah)* days

Sukkot Festival of Tabernacles, in October

Talmud Compendium of Jewish law, encompassing Oral Torah and regarded as divinely revealed; completed ca. 600 A.D.

Trefah Unfit, unclean, not ritually acceptable; opposite of *kosher*

Union Prayerbook Prayerbook of the Union of American Hebrew Congregations, reform movement in America

Wissenschaft des Judenthums Science of Judaism, modern scholarship in Judaic history and literature

Wunderrebbe Wonder-working rabbi

Yetzer Hatov Impulse to do good

Yetzer HaRa Impulse to do evil

Yichus Prestige, honor, repute, family distinction

Yiddish Jewish language formed of German, Hebrew, Polish, other Eastern European languages, ca. 1000 A.D.

Yidishkayt See *Jewishness*

Yizkor Memorial prayer for dead; May God remember . . .

Zaddik Righteous man, wonder-working rabbi in Hasidism

Zunz, Leopold German scholar, founder of scientific study of Judaism; 1794–1886

INDEX

INDEX